MEMORY TECHNIQUES FOR SCHOOL, WORK, & PLAY

By
John I. Caleb
&
Nicole Caleb

TABLE OF CONTENTS

CHAPTER 1	**HOW TO READ THIS BOOK (important)**	1
CHAPTER 2	**INTRODUCTION**	4
CHAPTER 3	**THE BRAINS RECORDING SYSTEM**	8
	ASSOCIATION	8
	IMAGINATION	8
CHAPTER 4	**USING IMAGINATION FOR ASSOCIATION**	11
	ASSOCIATION	11
	IMAGINATION	14
CHAPTER 5	**THE LINK SYSTEM**	16
CHAPTER 6	**THE PEG SYSTEM**	20
	DEVELOPING SPEED AND SKILL WITH YOUR PEGS	24
CHAPTER 7	**ADDITIONAL NOTES ABOUT THE PEG AND THE LINK SYSTEMS**	26
	EXTENDING A PEG LIST	26
	FORMING A CUSTOM PEG SET	28
	LINKING FROM PEGS	30
	MULTIPLE BRANCHING	31
CHAPTER 8	**THE LOCI SYSTEM**	34
CHAPTER 9	**THE STORY METHOD**	36
CHAPTER 10	**THE ALPHABET & OTHER CHARACTERS**	37
CHAPTER 11	**NUMBERS**	38
	NUMBER GROUPING	38
	REMEMBERING IT BACKWARDS	36
	USING THE LINK SYSTEM	38
	USING THE STORY METHOD	38
	USING THE PHONETIC NUMBER CODE SYSTEM	39
CHAPTER 12	**WORDS & NAMES**	40
CHAPTER 13	**PEOPLE**	42

CHAPTER 14	**THE PHONETIC NUMBER CODE SYSTEM**	44
CHAPTER 15	**NUMBERS WITH THE PHONETIC SYSTEM**	46
CHAPTER 16	**THE PHONETIC SYSTEM AS A PEG SYSTEM**	51
CHAPTER 17	**THE WEEKLY SCHEDULE**	53
CHAPTER 18	THE YEARLY SCHEDULE	56
CHAPTER 19	**DAYS OF DATES**	58
	FOR THE YEAR	58
	FOR THE CENTURY	60
CHAPTER 20	**TWO DIMENSIONAL PEGS WITH THE PHONETIC SYSTEM**	68
CHAPTER 21	**PLAYING CARDS**	69
	THE CARD ITEM	69
	IN A CARD GAME	70
	DETECTING MISSING CARDS	70
	MEMORIZING THE ORDER OF A SHUFFLED DECK	71
	DEVELOPING SPEED	72
	OTHER TYPES OF CARD DECKS	73
CHAPTER 22	**BINARY & OCTAL NUMBERS**	75
CHAPTER 23	**CODES**	82
	NUMBER CODE SYSTEMS	82
	MORSE CODE SYSTEMS	83
	BRAILLE	87
CHAPTER 24	**CHILDREN & GAMES**	90
	CONCENTRATION	95
	DICE AND DOMINOES	97
CHAPTER 25	**MISCELLANEOUS SYSTEMS**	103
	ACROSTICS	103
	ACRONYMS	104
CHAPTER 26	**SCHOOL & TECHNICAL SUBJECTS**	106

	VOCABULARY AND LANGUAGE	108
	HISTORY AND GOVERNMENT	110
	TYPING	111
	FOR THE COMPUTER TECH	114
CHAPTER 27	**SPEECHES, BOOKS, & STUDYING**	117
CHAPTER 28	**ARTIFICIAL & NATURAL ASSOCIATION**	121
	ARTIFICIAL ASSOCIATION	121
	NATURAL ASSOCIATION	121
CHAPTER 29	**MATHEMATICAL FORMULAS**	122
	FOR MORE COMPLEX FORMULAS	123
CHAPTER 30	**ADVICE**	132
	FORGETFULNESS PROBLEMS	135
CHAPTER 31	**THE GALLERY**	137
	ANSWERS TO EXERCISES	163
	BIBLIOGRAPHY	164
	ORDER FORM	165

CHAPTER 1

(*Important*)
HOW TO READ THIS BOOK

READ THIS BOOK I recommend that the reader pay the most attention to these first five paragraphs. Perhaps the reader should read these four paragraphs twice or more, and give every detail in them some thought. Therefore, attention to detail is important. In fact, attention to detail is very important for the lessons in this book.

As written in chapter 27 (*Speeches Books & Studying*), I suggest that when reading anything, for better comprehension, it's good to avoid reading too much at a time. Therefore, its better to read only a comfortable portion at a time, each with a comfortable interval of rest and reflexion on the portion just read.

I recommend that the reader pay the most attention to Chapters 4 through 11 (beginning on page 11). and Chapters 14 through 16. Almost all the techniques in this book are based on the contents of these chapters. Therefore, It is possible to **bypass** the other chapters, and yet obtain a sufficient knowledge. To **avoid** the boredom of Some of this chapter, and Chapters 2 and 3, you could reed this paragraph and the next two, then go directly to Chapter 4, to begin the lessons. In doing so, you'd probably be quite satisfied with what you obtain from this book. Most of the rest of the book covers various ways to can use whats taught in those lessons. To make it easier to find these essential pages, notice that in the Table of Contents, these chapters are in red letters, and that red tab markings are on the outer edges of the pages of those chapters, such as on this page. However, these pages so marked in red must be read and studied in consecutive order.

One reason I've contemplated bypassing certain chapters is that I realize that some subjects and subject matter in this book are not of interest to some people. Some of the subject matter is intended solely for (for example) college students in certain fields of study. However, in bypassing any of such, one could easily deprive oneself of useful tools and fun. Most of the systems are adaptable to other interests. Nevertheless, you can learn the other lessons at a later time of your choice. In addition, you can learn them in any order of your choice.

I want you now to think of yourself as you ask yourself the following questions:

- How much do I want to learn from this book?
- How good at memorizing things do I want to be?
- Am I willing to learn a new method even though I am satisfied with one I presently use instead, thus giving the new method a chance?
- Do I always assume that certain feats are impossible for me to do, even before I give them a good try?
- Do I assume that certain knowledge or subject matter is difficult for me to learn, even before giving it a good try?
- Would I assume that an idea or method new to me is impractical for my use, before I try it out well to see if it is so?
- Do I assume that certain knowledge or subject matter is useless for me?
- Do I assume that I will find certain knowledge or subject matter uninteresting, even before giving it a good look?

- Do I assume too much?
- Do I give up immediately if I don't succeed, or do I attempt to find out what I did wrong then try again?
- Do I allow the statements or opinions of another person cause me not to try out a method or idea?

If you honestly have a positive answer to each of these questions, you will be quite satisfied with what you gain from this book. If you don't, you must change those qualities at this point. However, don't worry because this is not difficult if you just give each of these questions an ample amount of thought.

You may find sometimes that a new way of doing something is initially more difficult than a way you had been doing it. However, if you become accustomed to the new method, you may find that it is much better than the old one. I want you to keep this in mind as you practice the techniques.

As for allowing the statements of another to stop you from trying a method or idea, I've written more about this in Chapter 30. Also in that chapter, is advice about testing the practicality of an idea or method new to you.

I've learned to avoid assumptions as much as I possibly can. Assumptions are the cause of all foolish actions. Therefore, I recommend that you consider all chapters. Some of these techniques may seem difficult at first, until you give them a chance. Then you will find them not so difficult after all. You should never give up immediately if you don't succeed in obtaining the desired results after following a set of directions. No matter now good any instructions are written, there is always the possibility that the reader has interpreted something wrong in them. This can happen to anyone. Therefore, instead of assuming that a certain method doesn't work for you, try to find out whether you've interpreted any or the instructions wrong or missed one or more details. Then you should try again.

To obtain anything from this book, you must have faith in it and in yourself. Again, don't always assume that a new task is impossible for you to do or difficult for you to learn. To avoid this sort of thoughts, just think of studying this book as discovering mental powers you never knew you always had. After all, it is true that you do have such abilities. I've written this book to show you so.

If you look through the pages of Chapters 5 and 6, you will see the words **Do it now** in bold letters. As you progress through these chapters and reach any of these points, closely follow the instruction just received at that point. You should not continue until you have completed the instruction. If you comply with this, you probably won't have any difficulty comprehending the rest of the book.

Also, throughout the book there are instructions to help one to comprehend the subject matter at hand. Such instructions usually begin with the words "For better comprehension,.. ."or something to this effect. Of course, I advise that you comply with them to assure that you comprehend the lesson at hand. This, I suggest you do even if you are sure that you understand well enough without it.

I intended to write this book in a way that people of all types can comprehend it. Therefore, some may find some of the text redundant and overly explaining. Never the less, I am not so concerned with this and composition as I am with the teaching of the memory techniques. Therefore, please bear this in mind as you proceed through this book.

There are but a few exercises in this book. The reason is that my intention is but to show you how. I leave it to you to provide for yourself your own practicing, testing and refinement of your skill at the techniques. The exercises in this book are necessary for comprehension. Nevertheless, I do provide methods and ideas for one to exercise and test one's self on all the lessons.

I suggest that you do practice and test the systems well, in order to realize their great effectiveness and potential. You can not realize how good the techniques are until you allow yourself to develop a bit of skill at them. Of course, I can tell you of 'the tremendous feats of memorization you can do after reading this book. However, I'm sure that you won't be impressed unless you see for yourself that it is true.

Therefore, I cannot prove to you that these techniques are as good as I say they are. This, you must do for yourself. To prove anything to oneself, one must be honest with oneself. One must know that one has done everything required and absolutely nothing less, and without any bias.

To instruct others in these techniques regardless of their age, the chapter of children and games (Chapter 24) contains excellent ideas.

CHAPTER 2

INTRODUCTION

This book is a lesson on the use of the brain's memory system in accords with its physical design. By not using the memory system in this way, a person's memory abilities are severely handicapped. Most people are not even aware of the great magnitude of their handicap in this category. Some of the same people consider themselves to be very good at memorization and this may even be true to some extent. Nevertheless, they still don't know what they are missing. Every person with a normal brain has tremendous memorization abilities that he or she probably is not even aware of. One objective of this book is to show you some of the awesome memory capabilities of your mental system. In this way, this objective is to eliminate these shortcomings permanently.

This book contains many amazing techniques that would make the task of memorizing just about any type of information much easier. One small example of the type of feats a person can do from the lessons in this book is: quickly and easily memorizing the order of a shuffled deck of playing cards after looking through the deck just once.

You will see that the techniques do not take much effort and development on your part as you might think. Many people have asked me such questions as:

- Do the techniques involve some sort of hypnosis or meditation?
- Do the techniques require much time to master?
- Can I easily forget the techniques and have to read this book again someday?
- Would I have to read many pages of the book in order to learn any of the fantastic feats you mentioned?

My answer to any of these questions is "absolutely not." When you see how the techniques work, you will also realize the they do make sense (I do not imply that Hypnosis and meditation doesn't make sense. I imply only that it doesn't to people who don't understand it.). You will probably wonder why you haven't thought of some of the methods yourself. You will also see that learning the techniques is like learning to ride a bicycle or learning to swim. Once you learn them, you will know them permanently. In the book, you will learn to do amazing feats of memorization, even in the first four chapters.

The techniques are fun to learn and use. Children as well as adults will find this to be so. For one reason, the techniques require and induce a broad use of the imagination. Therefore, they are entertaining to one who practices them. Because of this use of the imagination, they develop and exercise one's creativity. I've found that practicing the techniques and stunts will sharpen other mental functions as well.

People of almost all types would enjoy and benefit from knowledge in this book. These techniques are useful in everything you can think of that involves memorization. Let me give you some examples of some uses:

- To increase potential and success in school and test taking
- To increase job efficiency

- To increase ones' childrens chances of success
- To entertain others much like a magician does
- To impress others, such as your friends, your boss, customers, etc.
- To increase your chances of winning games such as card games
- To quickly learn a foreign language
- To exercise the mind, imagination, and creativity
- To increase efficiency in one's day to day life

Such is the reason for the name *Memory Techniques for School, Work, and Play*. I know that you have interests in one or more of the listed endeavors. Otherwise, you wouldn't be reading this now. Anyone who reads does have interest in one or more of those categories.

The average person should find the techniques very easy to master. I've found this to be so and I'm in this category. People may be skeptical if told of the stunts they can perform after reading this book. Even after a demonstration, people may still be skeptical of how easy they are to learn. I can understand this. For one reason, when I first learned one of the techniques, I could hardly believe the results. I still find the stunts I can perform somewhat incredible. Obviously, most people believe that only a few have such a gift, which does not include them. To this, I must say that I've learned never to judge my abilities before testing them.

For this book, I've done extensive research. In this book, I have conglomerated all the useful data I could find into less than 171 pages. If you glance through the table of contents, you would see that I've covered many subjects. I have used and performed every system and stunt in this book, and most of the details of the lessons I've learned from experience.

I discovered Memory Techniques about the year 1990 by taking a cassette tape course I ordered from a television advertisement. I ordered the course because at the time, I had problems memorizing, so much so, that I lost a good job as a result. I also ordered it because I was quite impressed by the demonstration of the course on television. As I tried the course, I soon found it quite effective indeed. I was so enthusiastic that I did further research on the topic. After reading other's books on the subject, I realized my own talent and knack, and therefore, decided to write my own book on it. I began the book in August of that year and completed it about a year later. However, in the time after-wards, before I could publish it, I've discovered more information useful and created many new innovations and contributions to the subject and to the book. One of these discoveries is my artistic talent. I therefore produced 24 drawings that I've included in this book. It was easy to include such innovations into the completed book because of the use of a modern computer. Therefore, the book has grown larger and better within the time I waited for the chance to publish it. I compare this book to the Grand Canyon, which is the result of many small changes and events over a long period of time. I don't wish to boast, however I see no other way to explain it.

My purpose in writing this book is to enlighten my fellow brothers and sisters of my discovery of Memory Techniques. Perhaps one or more of us will, with the knowledge from this book, take the topic to even higher scales and other dimensions. This subject could be raised to the level of a science. I for one can see that there are many more such techniques and improvements of such just waiting for someone to discover them. As I've said, I myself have invented many new innovations and improvements of the techniques, and this can be seen throughout the book. Because of this, it is evident to me that Memory Techniques are far from the development to their fullest potential.

I wish to mention now that there is a chapter in this book for children. I have a particular interest in the development of our young ones. We would all be much better off had we learned such techniques in our early childhood. Our minds would be much more organized and we would have a higher success rate. By now, the principles of the techniques would be embedded in our thinking. The techniques would in turn come into play without our even thinking of them. Nevertheless, with your continued use, you would obtain this in time.

Obviously, we have been deprived of the knowledge of such memory techniques. This lack of knowledge of them is the main reason that they have undergone such little development. Considering the many centuries Memory Techniques have been around, my opinion is that there should be much more sophisticated techniques available in this day and age. I'm sure that had Memory Techniques been more popular, many more people would have had the chance to contributed to their development.

This denial is either due to negligence of developers of our education system, or for all we know, it could have been intentional. Nevertheless, it is truly a crime that the education system has failed in this category. We all should have learned such techniques as part of our basic education. I feel that it should have been part of the junior high school and high school curriculums.

One observation I find unbelievable is that people with degrees in fields pertaining to psychology know very little of such memory techniques. This is the case with almost every such person I've spoken to about these techniques. I think that such memory techniques should have been an essential part of these fields of study at least. This further substantiates my premonition that the knowledge of such techniques has been purposely hidden from our society.

There could be quite a number of reasons for hiding such knowledge. This brings to mind, a book that pertains to the subject of controlling and altering the information and knowledge society receives. The name of the book is *Mind Control in the United States,* By Steven Jacobson. The book describes some facts I find quite interesting. Most I find quite logical, such as the following: The more one can control the information a group of people receive, the better and easier one can control that group of people. Another document of this category that I Find interesting is: The William Lynch Letter. This letter pertained to a manual for slave owners on methods and principles on how to maintain control of the slaves (I refer to slavery in America, and other surrounding countries, during the 1600s thru the 1800s).

With that said, I'll now return to the subject of this book. I do know that if such memory techniques were to suddenly become popular, it would drastically affect and change everything, especially the education system. This, of course, includes testing and teachers. In most cases, this would cause adverse effects initially. Nevertheless it would ultimately benefit us all.

The technical term for Memory Techniques is *Mnemonics*. The word is of ancient Greek origin. It is written that such techniques had been in extensive use in ancient times. This is likely because of the expense and lack of materials to write on, such as paper. Probably, as writing materials became more prevalent, mnemonics became less necessary, therefore less used. Probably as this occurred, their use became solely for entertainment such as vaudeville. Recently, the subject is becoming more popular. There are now television advertisements for taped courses on the subject, and many other books on this subject.

I've read about many famous people who were notorious for outstanding memory abilities. I've read that both George Washington and Napoleon could call by name each and every soldier in their armies. Also known for such abilities is Franklin D. Roosevelt, who happens to be related to Washington and ten other past presidents. I could name quite a few more individuals who were noted for such abilities and who held high positions.

I suspect that mnemonics has always been seriously taught and passed down among the families of such dignitaries. However, I do suspect that there are a few (very few) cases of which a person during childhood thinks of one or more of these methods and ideas unwittingly. This could have occurred because of some event or another, or a combination of such, in his or her life. Such people may not even be aware of this and the reason they have memorization abilities most others seem to lack. They may not even be aware that they are actually using such techniques as those in this book.

Now that I think of it, such people could be using techniques not even discovered yet. They may even have a way of thinking or reasoning, unknown in this society today. I believe that within ancient cultures and civilizations in such places as Africa, there had been such knowledge available to society. I am doing some research on this, to find out what of this is known. I've already learned of many innovations unknown by most of us. For instance, from the book *The Ankh,* By Nur Ankh Amen, I've learned about the use of electrical devices during ancient times. There are many books that contain interesting information about our ancient cultures as well of later times, that could even be purchased by street book vendors.

As for more recent times, one African American I've read about is Octave Rey. He was a police captain who served in New Orleans from the year 1868 to 1877. Supposedly, he had such good memory abilities that he could name each and every offender he saw, and he could do likewise with each and every citizen, including each child, of New Orleans. He had become quite an attraction to the city despite the great racism against people of color. He even served as state senator.

One great memory feat I think is worth including is that done by Benjamin Banneker, another African American. He was part of the team to design and build Washington DC, of which the blueprints involved many complex and intricate details. The man commissioned to design the city, for some reason became angry. Angry, he suddenly quit the job and left, taking all of the blueprints with him. This caused a great problem for those involved including George Washington. Banneker, who had seen all of the blue prints and plans, re-constructed all of them from memory. Thus, he saved the day.

There are many examples of fantastic memory feats within African culture. One that comes to mind is that of men called *Griots*. Griots have the task of mentally recording the history of a their tribe. Such a history usually goes back many centuries and consists of many details for each year. Such Griots appeared in the week long television movie *Roots*. This movie is one of the most popular of all American television movies of the time, which is during the year 1976.

CHAPTER 3

THE BRAINS RECORDING SYSTEM

As written in Chapter 1, One can still obtain a good knowledge from this book without reading any of this chapter. In this chapter, I discuss some aspects and concepts about the brain and memory. Therefore, I don't consider this chapter the beginning of the lessons. Never the less, to know and understand such aspects and concepts would be helpful to know of.

ASSOCIATION

When the brain records new information, it connects (associates) it with information previously recorded. The brain selects the most similar data to connect it to. The brain's memory system is a system that always tries to continue patterns already established in it. It is a system that creates and works with patterns. To recall information, the system looks to one or more of these patterns. To this system, new patterns are more obscure.

This is why you can memorize new information that makes sense to you more easily, than you could memorize such that doesn't. Take for example, a ten digit number. As you know, it is probably difficult to memorize. However, if the digits have a pattern that you can either recognize or derive some sense of, the number is much easier to memorize.

If there is no physical damage involved, a memory problem is not one of retention. It is one of recall. The brain never loses information. It always retains any information it ever receives. The problem is that one cannot always recall the data when one needs it. The brain's memory storage is like outer space, in which the desired data is somewhere out there. However it could be difficult to find among the vast darkness.

Of course in this vast darkness, there can be many individual bunches of information. Some are easier to find than others. For instance, one's own phone number is probably much easier to find in one's memory than another phone number one heard a day ago. However, it is possible to connect two or more bunches of information together. You can use this ability to organize all the bunches so that you can find any information easily.

As you probably know, one thought can remind you of another thought. In this book, you will learn how to associate two or more clumps of information together so that one will remind you of the others. This is especially useful on the difficult to find information.

IMAGINATION

In my opinion, this is among the greatest mental tools we were blessed with. It alone certainly separates us from all other species on earth. This book will show that it is an awesome tool to apply to memorization. What makes it such a tool is that with it, you can mentally link together, things that you otherwise cannot. I'm referring to things that you cannot derive or see any relationship to one another. This book is full of examples of the use of imagination to mentally link such together so that one can remind you of the other, or visa versa. As you read this book, bear in mind the ideas in this particular paragraph.

A recall problem can be solved by creating a new, more easily recallable, form of the information. Then to recall the information, you do not try to recall the original form of it. Instead, recall the new form of it then mentally convert it back to the original form.

As you probably know, it is much easier to recall an experience than it is to recall other forms of information. Examples of such other forms are, long digit numbers, codes, lists and charts. When considering evolution, the brain's memory system is most likely designed for experiences as opposed to these other forms of information mentioned. An experience can provide a multitude of connections (associations). You've probably heard the adage: *A picture is worth a thousand words.* An experience applies to all the senses simultaneously, whereas the other information forms do not.

This is where the use of imagination helps. For instance, information obtained by reading this page enters the brain by way of sight alone. The brain receives it as the sight of black printed words on white paper. However, using imagination, the mind creates images and such to add to this sight to make it meaningful, therefore more easily recallable. For instance, as you see the word "ammonia" you then imagine, thus form an image of, a bottle or puddle of ammonia. In addition, you imagine the sent of the ammonia. This is an example of two items added to the sight of that word on the paper. Throughout this book are methods that enable one to make optimum use of this aspect of the brain's system.

Imagination is the most essential element of memory and recall. After all, recalling is simply the act of thinking of something again. This is like bringing something out from memory storage. It is even more like going to storage and returning with a copy of that wanted from storage. Otherwise, the item would no longer be in storage, thus, never recallable ever after. Therefore, recall is basically a process of using imagination to re-create (or shall I say copy) into the present consciousness, information stored somewhere else. Take the example above about the ammonia. In order to think of a bottle of ammonia, one must imagine it, thus re-create it. Of course, the mind obtains the information needed for this from somewhere else in the brain.

Interesting experiences are easier to recall than uninteresting ones, which you probably know. Such an experience usually triggers one or more emotions. In doing this the experience draws the mind's attention, leaving a stronger impression in memory. Extraordinary experiences are almost always quite interesting.

One way to make a more easily recallable form of difficult information involves creating in your mine, an extraordinary experience. The elements in this created experience depict the details of the information. This you will learn to do with the use of your imagination. After all, a fantasy is but an experience created in the mind. A popular name for this technique is Imagery.

According to studies about the brain, the left hemisphere (side) of the brain controls such functions as logic, decisions, and judgment. The right hemisphere controls such functions as imagination and creativity. I like the explanation of this according to the book, *Metu Neter, Volume1*. It states the following:

```
In summary, let's note that the left hemisphere of the brain is
in charge of noting the difference between things, separating
wholes into parts, and enabling us to deal with all sequential
phenomena (wholes presented pieces at a time). This mode of
thinking is generally known as analytical, Cartesian, serial,
linear, deductive, segregative, etc. The right side is in charge
```

```
of noting the similarities between things, and their relation to
each other and the whole thus unifying them. This mode of
thinking is generally known as synthetical, holistic,
congregative, etc. We must also note that the left side of the
brain is extroverted and is therefore the means for the 'outer
culture' noted above. The right side is introverted and is the
means for the 'inner culture'.
```

Compared to the previous explanation, there is a strong similarity. Judgment does involve finding the difference between subjects, just as imagination and creativity does involve combining subjects. This does support my earlier statements about the use of imagination to link together, unrelated things. The creation of new things or ideas does involve combining already existing things or ideas. The book contains more information on this. I find the book remarkable and I highly recommend reading it.

I see an additional concept of this. It seems to me that the right side involves dealing with things that do not exist, and the left with things that do. This concept seems to agree with the others. Dealing with things that exist neither physically nor in one's mine, is in itself an act of mentally creating it. Dealing with things that do exist either physically or mentally does involves the use of judgment and reasoning.

In practicing the techniques, one developed the right side of the brain and its coordination with the left side. This is due to the extensive use of imagination. Therefore. One's imagination develops and improves. Imagination has the direct connection with creativity. Therefore one's creativity develops and improves as well. Such overall development also improves one's skill in anything learned from this book.

CHAPTER 4

USING IMAGINATION FOR ASSOCIATION

I advise you to pay the most attention to this chapter because it applies to everything in this book.

ASSOCIATION

In the lessons here, you will see how the imagination can be used to associate unrelated subjects. The use of such will be covered later. Therefore, I want you to work on learning the lessons here, without concern so much about the relevancy of it at this time.

Let's suppose that you want to mentally associate *book* with *telephone*. To do this, you could imagine a book and telephone interacting together. You do not want to imagine something boring, such as a book falling on a telephone. Such a boring experience, one would easily forget. Let's make it more bizarre. Let's make it ridiculous and impossible even. Remember, extraordinary, more interesting experiences are easier to recall.

You want to imagine something more interesting, such as:

 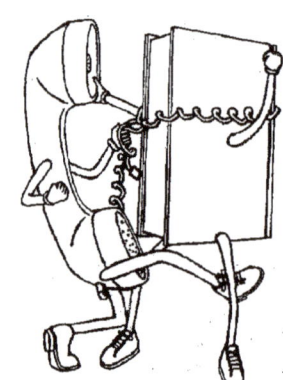

a book using a telephone   or   a book and telephone fighting

Some more examples are: telephones reading books in the library or people entering huge books used as telephone booths. More examples are: a telephone throwing books at you or:

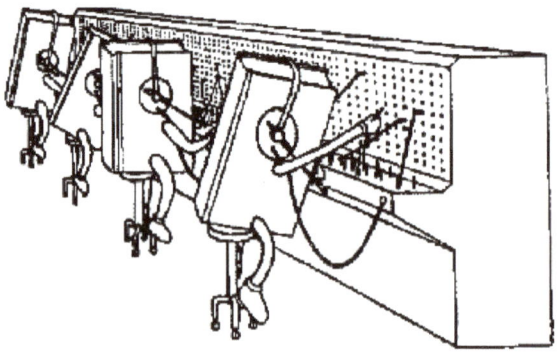

books working as telephone operators.

To mentally associate for instance *chair* with *baseball,* one could imagine something such as:

chairs playing baseball,

or baseball players using a large chair as the ball. What would you think of to associate these two items? You can use your imagination in this way to mentally connect (associate) two or more items so that one would remind you of the others. Throughout this book are memory techniques and systems that employ this idea. Therefore, I teach ways of using this type of mental associations to memorize vast amounts of data of all types. Therefore, you will learn how your imagination can be a powerful memorization tool.

Again, the more bizarre and out of context something is, the more easily you can recall it. This is very important for you to keep in mind throughout this book. For instance, to associate *ice cream* with *washing machine,* one might first think of something logical such as clothes soiled with ice cream and put into a washing machine. This scene is obviously uninteresting. Therefore, it is insufficient for our purpose here. One might even think of something a bit less logical, such as a large scoop of ice cream on the top of a washing machine. I admit that this is a scene unlikely to occur. However, it also lacks the needed aspects. It is boring. It is not incredibly bizarre and impossibly absurd. It will not stimulate the mind's interest. Therefore, it would not suffice for the memory techniques taught in this book.

Now let's take this scene and make it sufficient. To do this, one could imagine for instance that the scoop of ice cream suddenly grows to five feet tall and grows arms and legs. It then jumps off the washing machine, which has just grown its own arms and legs. Then both the ice cream and washing machine dance together splashing ice cream all over the place. Now this scene is definitely incredibly bizarre and impossibly absurd. It is much more interesting than before. I'm sure that you would agree that if you were to actually see this happen, you would never forget it. However, the scene as it was initially, you would easily forget.

Another sufficient scene for this is that of a scoop of vanilla and chocolate ice cream the size of a boulder rolling and bouncing around on top of washing machines. Just imagine actually witnessing something like this first hand. Do you think you could forget it?

The same principle applies whether a scene is one that actually happened or is one that you have created in your mind. You will more likely remember the more extraordinary scene. Therefore, make sure that the mental scenes you create for *Memory Techniques* are so bizarre that they could not possibly happen.

This may seem to be a contradiction to statements in the previous paragraph. One might think that such a ridiculous scene does not make sense. However, such a scene that you create for some specific purpose would make sense to you. This is so because you would know the reasons for each and everything in it. The scene would make sense to you, although it probably won't make sense to someone else. Then after a full explanation, it probably would make sense to someone else as well.

Throughout the book, I provide examples of bizarre images and scenes. However, you would find it much more effective to use your own ideas. For one reason, each person's mind is unique. This not only applies to your way of associating items, it applies to your images as well. The scene you imagine of, for instance, a book using a telephone would look very different from the scene that I've imagined. That is, had you not seen any illustration of my imagination of it.

I want you to really exercise your own imagination and creativity. This you must do in order to adequately benefit from this book. It is for this reason that the four pictures of this chapter are the only ones I have placed with the text that pertains to them. The rest of the pictures are in Chapter 30, on page 137, which I call, *the Gallery*. Of these, neither are they placed with their text, nor do I provide any reference to the location of their text. I've included such pictures merely to add color and interest to the book and to show off my art. I feel that such pictures could even be detrimental to your progress in this book if you don't exercise your own creativity.

You can sometimes use my examples and ideas when forming mental images. However, I advise that you form your own for your own development and progress. In addition, it is often better to use the first idea you think of. Changing ideas can cause confusion.

You may experience a bit of difficulty in forming ideas for such imaginary scenes and at times picturing them. Nevertheless, your mind is quite capable and equipped for this. If you give your mind a chance, it would always succeed at both of these tasks. In addition, such tasks would become even easier with continued practice.

For this, just remember not to restrict your imagination by trying to derive a logical image for associating two or more items together. Not only will this slow you down, this will undermine the effectiveness of the imaginary scene for Memory Techniques. Sometimes you might even immediately think of a more logical scene that joins the items. However, if this image is uninteresting and boring, it will not work well for Memory Techniques. Therefore a more bizarre and illogical joining of things is better. Just remember that it must not be boring to you.

Before we move on, I must tell you about two symbols you will see in the next chapter, as well as other chapters throughout this book. The two symbols are the following:

Look at them carefully please. Notice that each of these two symbols is a picture of two arrows entering a cloud and pointing at a chain linkage within. Each symbol depicts a linking together of the objects (words) the arrows are pointing from. These symbols depict such imaginary scenes as that I've just described. I will therefore refer to this symbol as a *linking scene* or a *linking image*. For an example of its use, to depict one of the scenes (drawings) that associates *book* with *telephone,* I will write it as follows:

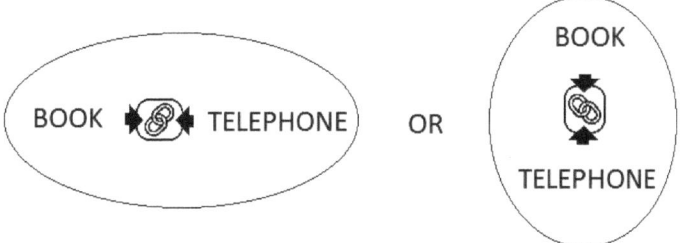

For another example, to depict a scene that associates jacket with cannon, I would write it as follows:

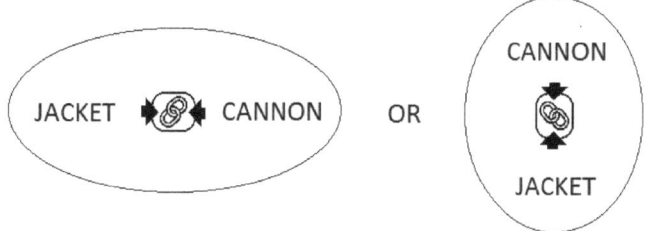

As you may see, the two words on either side of it, that the arrows point from, are the items placed into that scene. As I imply, I will be using such symbols throughout this book. I use it especially in the next three chapters, so keep it in mind.

IMAGINATION

You want the mental images you create to be as easy to recall as possible. You can significantly enhance your recall of such images by including a combination of the following aspects:

- Detail
- Color
- Action
- Other senses (sound, smell, touch, taste, etc.)
- Three dimensional view
- Emotions (comedy, anger, etc.)
- Exaggerations of size (extremely large or small)
- Exaggeration in quantity

Including the aspects listed above in the making of an imaginary image makes the image more noticeable. Thus, it is easier to find in memory. The more of these, and the more of each, you include, the better the recall power you will have of the image. It is like trying to spot an individual who is in a crowd. Obviously, you could spot the person more easily if he or she is wearing bright colors, jumping around, making noise, or doing a combination of such actions. Without such aspects, you would probably find the person difficult to spot.

Scenes that involve comedy and such are most likely unforgettable. As I've stated, an experience that triggers emotions leaves a stronger impression. The most effective scenes are those that make you laugh, or stimulate other enjoyable sensations (Are you thinking what I'm thinking? ☺) in you . You will find that any scene that accomplishes this always works well for Memory Techniques.

An example of a scene that includes exaggeration is that of a leather glove, that is as large as the Empire State Building, standing in the middle of the street where you live. Another is that of endless numbers of cats walking down your street. As you probably see, using exaggerations can make images more bizarre, and you don't have to limit the size of the images you imagine.

Of such images, don't imagine an image that is but a flat picture. Give the image three dimensions. Because of this idea, I use the term *scene* throughout this book instead of *picture*. A picture has but two dimensions. However, a scene has three dimensions and it could include all of the other senses. In addition, you can imagine yourself in a scene. Thus, the scenery can be all around you.

Make it a rule to include the top six always. I suggest that you experiment with the listed aspects to test their effectiveness. Throughout the book, I refer to this chapter, and it applies to this list especially. The main purpose of using the listed aspects is to make the image stand out in the scene you create. Also, apply detail to make the scenes look realistic, and not cartoon like. Make them as real in your mind as you can make them. Perhaps it would help to think of the phrase, "what would it be like if..." when forming such an imaginary image or scene.

The listed aspects that pertain to vision are most effective because sight has the most influence among all the senses. Hearing comes next after sight. People in general think in terms of sight more than any other of the six senses. Some clear indications of this are:

- Fear of the dark is extremely common.
- Of all the senses, the average person would fear the lost of sight the most by far.

Most likely, you agree with these two statements. As you will see, with the use of imagination, you can add all the listed aspects to any information to make it more memorable. This includes the aspect of vision.

Of the pictures in this book, they are but examples of the associations I've formed, in the way I've imagined them. As I've stated, yours would be different. In addition it is obvious that even if they had more color and detail, no such picture could include all the aspects of the list. Bear this in mind.

You must learn to form good mental images because you will be forming such images throughout this book. It is possible to form a good image within a minute amount of time, such as a split second. It is not time but a little concentration, which is what it takes to form a good image. I mention this because the use of the techniques sometimes require the ability to form images quickly. We will now begin with the learning of the systems. Now prepare for some fun.

CHAPTER 5

THE LINK SYSTEM

The Link System, also known as the Chain System, is used to quickly memorize a long list in a consecutive order. It employs all the principles in Chapter 4. To explain it, I will now apply it to a small shopping list as an example. Suppose that you want to remember to shop for the items of the following list, and in this particular order:

1. a dress shirt
2. an alarm clock
3. cookware
4. a sweater
5. a thermos bottle
6. an ironing board cover
7. a pencil sharpener
8. motor oil
9. a shower curtain
10. a bottle of whiskey

To apply the Link System, one would make the following imaginary scenes and in the following steps. Look this list over quickly and completely now. However, do not apply your imagination to it until instructed to do so (That is, until you've continued reading and thus, eventually arrive to the words "**Do it now**" in such green letters). (Yes, obviously I'm trying to avoid your proceeding ahead before receiving important instructions). Observe the scenes (depicted by the *linking scenes* symbols) which descend down in the center of the right (imaginary scenes) column. Notice the structure of the list and how it applies to the list above.

STEPS	IMAGINARY SCENES		
1.	dress shirt	🔗	alarm clock
2.	alarm clock	🔗	cookware
3.	cookware	🔗	sweater
4.	sweater	🔗	thermos bottle
5.	thermos bottle	🔗	ironing board cover
6.	ironing board cover	🔗	pencil sharpener
7.	pencil sharpener	🔗	motor oil
8.	motor oil	🔗	shower curtain
9.	shower curtain	🔗	whiskey

To begin, you create in your mind the scene in step 1. That scene associates *dress shirt* with *alarm clock*. To form that scene, you could imagine for example, a giant alarm clock trying to put on a dress shirt.

You then move down to step 2. to form the next scene. That scene associates *alarm clock* with *cookware*. To form that, you could imagine a scene such as an alarm clock chased by some cookware. Just imagine for example what that clock and cookware looks and sounds like running around on a friend's kitchen floor.

In step 3, you mentally form a scene associating *cookware* with *sweater*. For that, you could imagine a scene of, for instance, people walking the streets wearing sweaters made of regular sized cookware instead of wool. Yes, imagine the clanging sounds these people probably make as they swing their arms back and forth.

For step 4. (sweater with thermos bottle), you could imagine a scene of for instance, relatives wearing sweaters made of thermos bottles of assorted sizes and colors. Just think of it. By putting hot beverages into the thermoses, they can carry some of their lunch around with them as well as keep themselves warm. Of course such sweaters are probably very bulky.

Of course, you continue forming such imaginary scenes, thus continuing until you've done all 9 steps. Again, these scenes and images are but examples. You can use these ideas or come up with your own.

In following the steps just mentioned, you would have made **nine different separate** imaginary scenes. Be careful not to include all the items of a scene into the next scene. For instance, don't include dress shirt into the scene of step 2. Likewise, don't include alarm clock into that of step 3, and so forth. Therefore, each imaginary scene is to contain but two of the listed items. Now take your time and, while observing the lists above, form all the imaginary scenes from step 1. to step 9 (remember to apply the lessons on imagination in chapter 4.). If you wish to, when forming a scene, close your eyes to focus. Do it now.

To recall the list, begin by simply thinking about the image you imagined of the first item, *dress shirt*. This would remind you of the second item (alarm clock) since it is combined with it in the same scene. Then think of the other alarm clock. This would automatically bring to mind the next scene (alarm clock with cookware). Then think of the other set of cookware. This in turn brings to mind the next scene (cookware with sweater). Then think of the other sweaters, and so on. Close the book and in this manner and order, recall the entire list. **Do it now**.

If you had any difficulty recalling anything here, don't worry. Your problem is probably that you didn't always apply the lessons in Chapter 4 well enough, and this is normal in the beginning. With a little practice and review, this would cease to be a problem. As you continue in this chapter, you will encounter more such lists for your use in practicing the link system. Therefore you will have another chance to try it. Once you do it correctly, you would never have such difficulty with it again because, as I've said, it is like learning to ride a bicycle. If you feel that you did not do excellently in the attempt to recall the list, I want you to review Chapter 4. As you review it, look for aspects of those lessons there that you could have applied better in this attempt at the Link System. **Do it now**.

As you might already surmise, my reason for the instruction before, that you not apply imagination until further notice, is to help assure that you place the proper items in each scene, and also the proper amount (two items in each) in each scene (Yes, I have encountered, one or more persons of which this were a problem).

It is important that you become good at the Link System to effectively comprehend the book. This chapter and Chapter 4 are the most crucial chapters. You should not continue to the next chapter until you are confident with the Link System. Therefore, you should practice it well before leaving this chapter.

As you become familiar with the Link System you would see, that each scene reminds you of the next scene. Therefore, one can say that each scene is linked to the next. The following is another way to display the list of scenes of the example I just used:

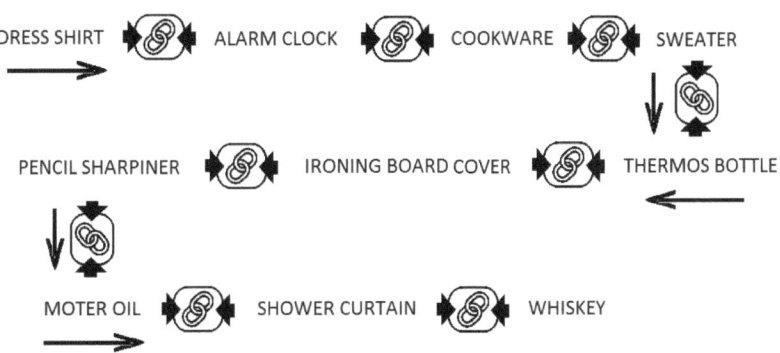

Notice the linking scene symbols. Again, each linking scene symbol depicts the imaginary scene that joins the two items it is in-between. As you can see, the series begins at the top left, goes toward the right, goes down, then proceeds toward the left, goes down, then goes right. In fact, it forms a large reversed S shape. Isn't it like a chain? Therefore, the name Link System is appropriate. Notice that there are nine scenes (the symbols) in this structure as well. The diagram above clearly shows that each item links one scene to another. This is the structure I will use throughout the book to depict the Link System from now on.

Try using the scenes you've created in your mind to recall the list backwards. To do this, you begin with the last scene, which is the scene with the whiskey. You then use this scene to recall the previous scene. Then you use this previous scene to recall the scene preceding it, and so on. You would find that the links also work in reverse.

Here, I used but a ten item list. Nevertheless, you would find that this system works just as easily for lists of much longer lengths. One of the best ways to sharpen your skill in the use of imaginary images is to practice this system on long lists in both directions.

The best way to practice this system is simply to use it. Nevertheless, another way is to apply it to memorizing a list of items from a large department store catalog. For example, one could practice by memorizing, for instance, all third items of each page of the catalog.

I've made the following lists for you to practice the Link System on. Use the Link System to quickly memorize and recall backwards and forwards the following two lists.

1. door mat
2. turpentine
3. smoke screen
4. turkey
5. seashell
6. boxing glove
7. typewriter
8. tomb stone
9. marshmallow
10. Toyota
11. apple turnover
12. guitar
13. mushroom
14. ashtray
15. spot light
16. cement
17. pirate
18. donkey
19. siren
20. scarf
21. biscuit
22. elephant
23. detergent
24. fish net

1. cattle	7. cat	13. samurai	19. pipe organ
2. candle	8. rooster	14. baby crib	20. walrus
3. cassette	9. doctor	15. blender	21. ballerina
4. crayon	10. vacuum cleaner	16. mosquito	22. lizard skin
5. mud	11. lumber	17. razor	23. flashlight
6. phasor	12. dinosaur	18. ice burg	24. soda pop

CHAPTER 6

THE PEG SYSTEM

The Peg System, also known as the Hook System, enables one to learn or recall a list in any order. To describe it, I will now show how to make and use a very small set of what I call, number pegs. In this chapter, the set is very small for the sake of simplicity in explaining this system.

The first task, which is to make a set of such pegs, is to construct a numbered list of items in which each item would remind you of its number. The following are two such lists:

This is a list of items that resemble their numbers.

- 0. donut
- 1. tree trunk
- 2. swan
- 3. flying sea-gull
- 4. sailboat
- 5. dangling hook
- 6. tuba
- 7. street lamp
- 8. hour glass
- 9. lasso (cowboy rope)

This is a list of items that rhyme with their numbers.

- 0. Pharaoh
- 1. gun
- 2. shoe
- 3. key
- 4. door
- 5. hive
- 6. sticks
- 7. heaven
- 8. skate
- 9. sign

As one can see in the lists above, a 0 does resemble a donut, as a 4 resembles a sailboat. Gun rhymes with one, as skate rhymes with eight, and so on. Therefore, each item would easily remind you of its number. Therefore, it should be easy to memorize either of these lists. I could have made lists that range from 1 to 10 instead of from 0 to 9. I have a reason for the numbering to be as it is of the lists above, which I will explain later.

The next task is to set up such a list as a number peg system. To describe this procedure, it doesn't matter which peg list I use now. Nevertheless, I will use the list that rhymes. For this set up, I want you now to learn well the list that rhymes. Learn it well enough to say it in and out of order. **Do it now**.

Now form a scene of each of the rhyming items in its natural surroundings. For examples, the scene of the gun could be that of a rifle range, and the scene of the shoe could be that of a shoe repair shop or in a shoe store. Again, apply the lessons in Chapter 4. Make each item very noticeable in its scene. You can make the items bizarre if you wish to. There is to be but one listed item to a scene. Therefore, when you have finished, you will have formed ten scenes. Take your time and mentally form the ten scenes. **Do it now**.

Your setup is now complete. I will now show how to use these ten scenes to memorize a numbered list of random items. Thus, this set of scenes becomes a tool for easily memorizing any other list. For this, let's apply the scenes to memorizing the following random list:

0. Rolls Royce
1. egg shell
2. chopsticks
3. helicopter
4. Saturn
5. paddle
6. light-bulb
7. bubblegum
8. buffalo
9. dragon

To apply, you would make the following associations using the ten scenes you've just made. You are to place each of the random items into the appropriate scene. View the following list quickly and thoroughly now. However, again do **not** apply your imagination to it until instructed to do so. Therefore, do not apply it until you've continued reading and reached the words, "do it now" in such green letters.

STEPS	IMAGINARY SCENES	
	Rolls Royce	Pharaoh
	egg shell	gun
	chopsticks	shoe
	hellicopter	key
	Saturn	door
	paddle	hive
	light bulb	sticks
	bubble gum	heaven
	buffalo	skate
	dragon	sign

Again, I use the *linking scene symbol* in each row to depict each imaginary scene. For example, for the scene at the very top, you could imagine that in the scene you created of the Pharaoh, instead of human servants, Rolls Royces are bowing up and down before him. For the next scene below it, which is the scene with the gun or guns, imagine that you, or someone else, are shooting a gun that is made of broken egg shells. Just imagine the feel of the egg yolk dripping down onto the fingers wrapped around that gun. Also, the shells are quite fragile and delicate in hand. Again, these are but examples of what to think up.

As you probably have noticed, I didn't number the steps this time as I did for the Link System. Instead, I left the steps column blank. The reason for this is that with the Peg System, the sequence of steps is optional. For instance, you can do the association of the bottom row (*dragon* with *sign*) before that of that in the row of *helicopter with key*, which you could do before that of *paddle with hive,* and so forth. Therefore, you can form these associations in any order you wish. Therefore, you could place the numbers (from 1 to 10) in the steps column in any order you wish to, then form the imaginary scenes in the order you've chosen.

Now, using a **random** order as if randomly numbering the steps in the steps column, use the imaginary scenes you've created in the setup to form all the ten associations above. Remember to apply the principles in Chapter 4. Do it now.

Now look it over again quickly to make sure that you haven't missed any.

Now, to recall for instance item eight of the random list, simply think of the scene of the item that rhymes with eight, which is skate. You would of course see in that scene, item eight interacting with it. To recall item number four, think of the door. To recall item number nine, think of the sign, and so on. Therefore, one can also recall in any order one wishes to. This also works in reverse. For example, to recall which number is assigned to helicopter, think of the helicopter you had imagined. Close the book and in this manner, recall all the random items from 0 to 9. **Do it now**.

As you probably surmise, my reason for the instruction before, that you do not apply imagination until further notice, were so that you would have had more of a tendency to try it using a random order of steps, as suggested, before going ahead and applying imagination before reading further (Yes, I've encountered persons who, because of enthusiasm, had proceeded ahead in this way, before my completing my instructions).

One could call a peg system a mental filing system. Notice that each of the ten scenes you created in the setup is used like a numbered file folder in your mind. The most popular concept and explanation of the peg system (the explanation and terminology used in other books I've found on this subject), is that it is named the peg system, because using it is like hanging the random items on a row of labeled pegs or hooks. In the example we've used, the labels are the items that rhyme. However, I myself do not think of the peg system in this way. Therefore, I would not have chosen such a name for this system. I prefer instead, the name, labeled scenes (not pegs nor hooks). Nevertheless, from this point on throughout the book, I will refer to them as pegs. This, I do for accordance with the terminology of other books, and for convenience (because peg is but a one syllable three letter word). Also, throughout the book, I've occasionally placed the word scene in parenthesis next to the word peg. This, I did to help remind the reader of this particular paragraph. Yes, I think it's beneficial to bare in mind what's said in this paragraph while reading this book. This brings to mind a paragraph on page 15, that contains much about the advantages and features of a scene, when compared with a picture. This brought to mind, thoughts and ideas about one of the devices featured in many episodes of the television series, *Star Trek the Next Generation*. One of the space ships in this series is named, the *Enterprise*. In the *Enterprise*, is a room called, The *Holo-deck*. The *Holo-deck* is a room in which the ships computer can create and generate just about any scene and situation, along with its corresponding objects, creatures, people, action, etc. The potential size and dimensions of such scenes, along with any objects and such included in the scenes. seem to be limitless. The Holo-deck is used for entertainment, solving problems (for example, simulating a situation in order to help solve a problem), etc. For examples, in the *Holo-deck*, one or more crew members can sail a boat in the sea, go horse back riding in a forest, experience & act in a movie, etc.

Therefore, to help understand the peg system, one can think of these pegs (scenes) as a series of such *Holo-decks*. **Yes**, imagine a hallway with a series of doors of which each is the door of one of these *Holo-decks* (each room different inside from any other in the series, of course), such as this picture:

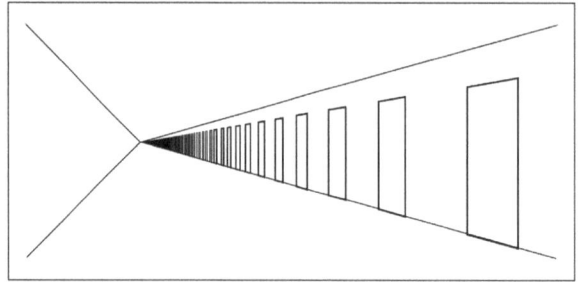

Yes, imagine that there are 100 rooms, and that each door has a number on it, and that the numbers range from 0 to 99. Imagine also, that of each room, the scene within reminds you of the number on its door. I'd bet that you can now figure out how to use this idea to aid in understanding the peg system.

As I've said at the beginning of this chapter, here, I'm using very small lists to explain the peg system. Nevertheless, using the peg system, you could even apply a list of 100 or more, and just as easily. That is, provided you have that many pegs. Other chapters in this book do cover both ways to form larger peg sets, and more efficient peg systems.

Also as stated at the beginning of this chapter, I call the type of peg set described in this chapter, a number peg set. I call it this because the peg labels depict numbers. Nevertheless, there are other types of peg sets of which the labels do not depict numbers. The labels could depict other characters such as, letters of the alphabet, or months of the year, and so forth. There are such examples in this book. As you progress, you will find them if you look for them.

The items placed into pegs are removable and changeable. Therefore, pegs are reusable. To learn this well, I want you now to do the following exercise. I want you to change the items in pegs 1, 4, 5, and 6 to the following:

1. brick

4. telephone

5, sewing machine

6. fire engine

For example, to change the item in peg 1. to brick, you could simply imagine that all of the eggshells in that scene suddenly turn into bricks. Imagine how heavy those bricks are. Again, the labels, must never be removed. Now, applying the lessons of Chapter 4, change the four items. Do it now.

Next, I want you to recall the entire list descending from 9 to 0. **Do it now**.

You probably now realize that you have indeed changed those items. With the use of this method, you can reuse the entire peg set. A scene can have more than two items in it by simply having all the items interacting with one another. There are examples of this throughout this book, and in the next chapter. I prefer a limit of five items to a scene. The list of items that resemble their numbers is useful with different languages. Unlike the rhyming list, one would not have to change the objects to apply it to another language.

Combining the two peg lists on page 20 would form twenty pegs. For example, you could use the list that rhymes for pegs 0 to 9, and the other list for pegs 10 to 19. Thus, you could form the following set:

0. pharaoh	10. donut
1. gun	11. tree trunk
2. shoe	12. swan
3. key	13. flying see-gull
4. door	14. sailboat
5. hive	15. dangling hook
6. sticks	16. tuba
7. heaven	17. street light
8. skate	18. hour glass
9. sign	19. lasso

Notice that the first ten is from the second peg list on page 20. The next ten (10 to 19) is from the first peg list on that page. Notice that of the numbered items after item 9, I simply took that first list from that page and added ten to each number, or simply placed a 1 to the left of each digit. Now you probably see why I made peg lists that range from 0 to 9 instead of from 1 to 10. These lists are more convenient for doubling the number of pegs in this way. You will see the convenience of this in the next chapter as well.

Now learn well the first peg list on page 20. Learn it well enough to say it in and out of order. **Do it now**.

Now learn well the new peg set above. **Do it now**.

Using this new list, you could apply a list of 20 items as easily as you have just done the list of ten items. I now want you to do an exercise of this. I want you to apply the following list of random items to pegs 10 to 19 of the new peg list above:

10. football	15. rain cloud
11. tooth paste	16. piano
12. spider	17. aspirin
13. tractor	18. cupcake
14. organ grinder	19. swimming pool

Now place each random item above into its correct peg. **Do it now**.

Now close the book and mentally review all of the pegs from 0 to 19. **Do it now**.

Of course, it would have worked just as well had you made the rhyming list the one from 10 to 19, and the other list the one from 0 to 9 instead.

One way of practicing this system is to have others make up numbered lists to recite to you in random order. Then you are to call out the names to the numbers they call out and sometimes the numbers to the names. You would probably impress them with this demonstration.

DEVELOPING SPEED AND SKILL WITH YOUR PEGS

For this, I recommend making up a set of flash cards. The number of flash cards in this set is of course your choice. Each card is to have on it a different number ranging from 0 to the number of cards there is. Therefore, if there were one hundred cards, then the numbers would range from 0 to 99.

To use this set, you shuffle them up, then you look at each card one by one until you've looked at them all. As you proceed, you are to look at each cards number. When looking at a number, you are to try to recall the peg (imaginary scene) of that number.

This, I recommend practicing periodically. As time goes on, your speed and dexterity at using your pegs will increase more and more.

I've also found it useful (while doing the exercise just mentioned) to (upon seeing a card's number) either look away from the cards (or close your eyes) immediately after seeing the number, then announce the number either aloud or mentally, then attempt to recall its peg (scene), before proceeding onto the next card. However, I recommend using this procedure after you've become confident with the peg set you're applying this to.

I prefer making my card set by printing such numbers on the front of regular playing cards, because playing cards are easy to shuffle and they are durable. Of course a card deck would suffice for only as much as 54 pegs (and this does include the two jokers). However you could increase the number of pegs by adding more cards from another deck. Perhaps the math flash cards for children would suffice for such a purpose.

I've even taken this method a step further. As I've said, on the face side of each card is a number I've printed. However, on the other side, the back side, of each card, I've clearly written a word or two that describes the peg (scene) of that number that's on the other side. With this, I can instead practice recalling each number to the peg description I see. Of course this is done by doing the exercise while looking at the backs of the cards instead of their fronts.

Never the less, it pays to practice both. That is, recalling the numbers to pegs, and recalling pegs to numbers. I recommend alternating the two, and giving each the same amount of practice.

I've recently learned that there are now flashcard programs and software available to use on such electronic devices as: smart-phones, I-phones, I-pads and tablets, laptops, etc. Such methods can be used instead of the use of such paper cards as described in this sub-chapter. In addition, some of these programs are free of charge. I've recently downloaded a few of these programs into three such electronic devices of my own, tested them, then selected one of them as my favorite.

CHAPTER 7

ADDITIONAL NOTES ABOUT THE PEG AND THE LINK SYSTEMS

It is to your advantage to mentally establish at least two peg systems of which each consists of about 100 pegs. For this, I recommend that you use some of the methods taught in this chapter to establish in mind additional peg systems. As you will see in a later chapter, I've included in the book many fun games to play. Some of the games are very good for mentally establishing new peg sets.

I recommend that you familiarize yourself with all methods in this chapter, before choosing any of them.

EXTENDING A PEG LIST

Of the first two methods I cover here, this paragraph explains the main principle of both of these methods. Both methods are alike in structure. Of these methods, you form another set of pegs to add to the set. To select each new peg label, you use one of the labels of the original set as an example. In the lessons here, I will call a label's example its counterpart. The Rhyming Peg System of Chapter 6 consists of ten pegs. Therefore, when applying that system to these methods, each new label is ten higher than its counterpart. For examples, The counterpart of label 10 is label 0. That of label 11 is label 1. That of label 17 is label 7. That of label 13 is label 3, and so forth.

One method works as follows. To double the number of pegs, you can form pegs of which the labels are made of a material different from that of their original counterparts. In addition, each new label is made of this material. For example, labels 10 to 19 could be items made of, for instance, paper. Thus, label 10 is a paper pharaoh (Yes, you are to imagine a pharaoh made of paper instead of flesh, bones, and blood.) In turn, label 11 is a paper gun, label 18 is a paper skate, and so forth.

You can add as many pegs as you want using this method. To add ten more pegs, you can label scenes 20 through 29 with items made of, for instance, glass. To add more, labels 30 to 39 could be made of, for instance chocolate, and so forth.

The following is a table showing these examples:

0 pharaoh	10 paper pharaoh	20 glass pharaoh	30 chocolate pharaoh	40____pharaoh
1 gun	11 paper gun	21 glass gun	31 chocolate gun	41____gun
2 shoe	12 paper shoe	22 glass shoe	32 chocolate shoe	42____shoe
3 key	13 paper key	23 glass key	33 chocolate key	43____key
4 door	14 paper door	24 glass door	34 chocolate door	44____door
5 hive	15 paper hive	25 glass hive	35 chocolate hive	45____hive
6 sticks	16 paper sticks	26 glass sticks	36 chocolate sticks	46____sticks
7 heaven	17 paper heaven	27 glass heaven	37 chocolate heaven	47____heaven
8 skate	18 paper skate	28 glass skate	38 chocolate skate	48____skate
9 sign	19 paper sign	29 glass sign	39 chocolate sign	49____sign

Observe some of the boxes of the table above. Each box contains a number with the peg label that represents it. Each column has ten of the pegs in consecutive order. Observe some of the rows going from left to right and notice the pattern of the numbers and labels. The numbers increase in tens and the leftmost label is the original counterpart of the other labels in that row.

Take box 22. To form that peg, one could imagine for example, a scene of Cinderella's glass slippers. To form peg 25, one could imagine for example, a scene of bee hives in trees and made by bees, and of which the bees have built into them, large glass windows so that their queen bees can watch outside activity. To form peg 34, one could imagine a scene of the chocolate door of the witch's gingerbread house in the story *Hansel and Gretel.* Now I want you to look at some of the other boxes and form mental scenes to be those pegs. When using this method, I advise that you make the labels and scenes look different from the other of that row.

In the fifth column, there are blank lines next to the numbers. I included this fifth column to show that you could extend the pegs to as many pegs as you want. On these blank lines, you could write the name of a new substance of your choice. For instance, you could write *rubber* on each line. Thus, you would form more peg labels. To form even more, just make an additional column such as the fifth column, with numbers from 50 to 59. Then use another substance such as copper, and so forth. Another variation of this idea is to use an adjective other then a substance. For example, you could write the word frozen or molten on each line.

You could more quickly and easily memorize such a table if you could easily recall which substance pertains to which column, or visa versa. To help with this, you could use one of the basic peg sets on page 20. The following is an example:

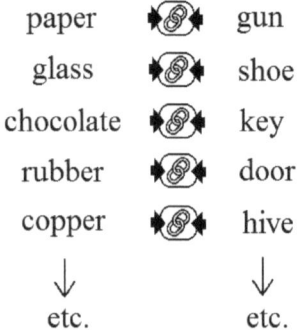

Compare this list with the table above. If you do, you would see a correspondence of the table's columns, with numbers 1, 2, and 3 of the list just above this paragraph. I've added 4 and 5 to the list in an attempt to show that this method is useful on tables consisting of many more columns as well. As you can see, the lines of the list correspond to the columns of the table. The very top line pertains to the teens column. The next line below pertains to twenties column, and so forth.

You probably already see how you could use the list in memorizing the table. Never the less, I will now show an example. Suppose that you wish to recall the peg name of peg 36. Because the first digit of the number 36 is 3, you could recall from line 3 of the list above (which you are to memorize by use of a peg system) that substance number 3 is *chocolate*. Then because the second digit in 36 is 6, you would put the word *sticks* next to the other word, to derive *chocolate sticks*. It's that simple.

Now for the other extension method. Of this method, you form peg labels that you can easily relate to their counterparts. For example, I would choose Moses as peg label 10. The reason is that Moses is the first thing I would think of if I think of pharaoh. For 11, I would use something I relate to *gun* such as *bullet*, or *cannon*. For 13, I might use something such as *acorn* or *nest* and so forth. To make ten more pegs, I form a new list that relates to items of the second list. For example, for label 20, I might use *tablets* because that is what I relate to *Moses*.

If I were to use this method and make a chart, it might look like the following:

0 pharaoh	10 Moses	20 tablets	30 note pad	40____
1 gun	11 cannon	21 civil war	31 slave	41____
2 shoe	12 leather	22 plastic	32 petroleum	42____
3 key	13 safe	23 guard	33 soldier	43____
4 door	14 window	24 curtain	34 skirt	44____
5 hive	15 sting	25 needle	35 sewing	45____
6 sticks	16 log	26 fireplace	36 radiator	46____
7 heaven	17 church	27 preacher	37 politician	47____
8 skate	18 ski	28 snow	38 rain	48____
9 sign	19 store	29 cash register	39 calculator	49____

As you can see, each item in the table was derived from the item to its left. For instance, for 26, I look at 16. For that, *fireplace* is the first thing I would think of if I think of *log*.

If you have difficulty recalling the peg of a particular number, you simply think of its counterpart, which is of course ten less than that number. In the table, it is the peg to the left of it. This method of recall, you use until you have firmly established in mind all such details of the new pegs. Then the use of this way of recalling the labels would no longer be necessary and you would have mentally established the new group of pegs.

There is one small problem with this system. Trying to establish in mind a large number of new pegs at a time can be very confusing. Therefore, you should not form new pegs until you have memorized well the latest group of pegs. You should repeat this process in multiples of only ten or twenty at a time.

FORMING A CUSTOM PEG SET

I myself like this method best of all among others in this chapter. You can use as a number peg set, any numerical list of scenes you can conjure up and memorize in a set order. Throughout the book, there are many examples of this. For example, my number peg set consists of lists of all kinds of subjects such as, siblings, past girlfriends, planets, past grade school teachers, the spouses of my siblings, movie monsters, the six chess pieces with three of the four card suits, *The Ten Commandments,* etc. For such a use, I find it best to choose lists of which each list already has an easily recognizable order that I'm already familiar with. Notice the examples I've such mentioned. For example, the order of the siblings would of course be according to age (I myself have the fortune of having seven brothers and sisters and two parents, therefore, I have the perfect amount for this use.). The order of the nine planets of our solar system would be according to distance from the sun, The order of past school teachers would range in order from kindergarten to the ninth grade, and so forth.

For examples of peg ideas, for the knight (chess piece), I've chosen a scene of the knights at the round table in the movie, *Ex Caliber.* For the queen (chess piece), I've chosen a scene in a movie of which actor Bette Davis is Queen Elizabeth. For the planet Mercury, I chose a scene in a television commercial of which the Greek god Mercury is running while holding a bouquet of flowers. For the planet Saturn, I imagine a scene of being close to and on its rotating rings. For the Earth, I chose a scene in the movie, *When Worlds Collide,* a movie of which the Earth is about to end. For the planet Neptune, I imagine a scene of the Greek God of the sea, Neptune. For the first commandment I've chosen the scene in the movie, *the Ten Commandments* of which Moses encounters the burning bush. For the ninth commandment I've conjured up a scene of which Moses is conducting a trial for a person, to determine whether the person has born false witness against his neighbor. For the eighth commandment (Thy shall not steel), I've chosen a scene in the same movie. It is a scene of which one of the Hebrews, moments before the Exodus, is handing out spoils of Egypt.

For the movie monster list, I've chosen an order according to characteristics of the monsters. For example, I choose *the Mummy* as monster zero because he probably was a Pharaoh (rhymes with zero). I choose the cyclops as monster one, because he has but one eye. The *War of the Worlds* martian is monster three, because he had three eyes and he counted and did everything in threes. Monster five is *Thing* in the *Adams Family* television series. *Thing* was but a gloved hand that appeared on the show by popping up out of drawers and boxes then interacted with the other characters of the show. Of course, I chose *Thing* as monster five because of its five fingers. I could easily continue mentioning more examples.

One can use a basic peg set, such as one of the two lists on page 20, as an additional aid in memorizing all such lists. The following is an example of such a use (Yes, you probably notice my list of siblings in the example):

PEGS 0 THRU 9		PEGS 10 THRU 19		PEGS 20 THRU 29	
Sun	Pharaoh	Dad	Pharaoh	_____	Pharaoh
Mercury	gun	Lisa	gun	_____	gun
Venus	shoe	Lessie	shoe	_____	shoe
Earth	key	Abe	key	_____	key
Mars	door	John (me)	door	_____	door
Jupiter	hive	Vernell	hive	_____	hive
Saturn	sticks	Ombu	sticks	_____	sticks
Uranus	heaven	Horretta	heaven	_____	heaven
Neptune	skate	Yvonne	skate	_____	skate
Pluto	sign	Mom	sign	_____	sign

Again, I use the linking scene symbol to depict any imaginary scene in the chart. For an example, of the use of this aid, I've applied it to peg 15 by associating my sister Vernell with hive (for five). For this, I imagined that she is being chased around her back yard by a bee hive and its bees, while the queen bee sits and rides on the hive shouting, "get her, get her,...!". To associate, for example, my sister Yvonne with skate (for eight), I imagined her skating around and break dancing while in her living room. Using such a method, I can easily recall, for example, that my sister Yvonne is peg 18. for one reason, it's already easy enough to remember that my siblings are in the set of teens (10 thru 19). For another reason, I've mentally associated her with skate (for eight). This method can be used to help in memorizing *the Ten Commandments* in the correct order. That is of course, if you don't already know it.

As you probably surmise, the reason for the blank lines in the series from 20 thru 29, is that the choice of list is optional. Likewise, the choice of list from 30 thru 39 is optional, and so forth.

To use this aid I suggest that you first form each peg (scene) without the aid (the rhyming list). Therefore, of the scene I mentioned of my sister Vernell. I first imagined her in her back yard without the hive and bees. Then to help in recalling her assigned peg number. I then mentally added the hive and bees to this scene. Therefore, if ever you have difficulty recalling the number to any particular peg (or the peg to a particular number), you then apply the corresponding rhyming item to that peg. Therefore, you can apply this method to help in memorizing each and all pegs.

The more you become accustomed to using any of your peg set, the more easily you will be able to recall the peg number of any of your pegs or the peg of any number within the whole set, and without the need for the aid (the rhyming list). Thus, the pegs will eventually become firmly established in mind. How fast this occurs is up to you and the amount of practice.

LINKING FROM PEGS

You can combine the Link System with the Peg System. The item placed into a peg can be the beginning of a series of linked scenes. To demonstrate this technique, I will now apply it to the rhyming list as is was applied to the very first random list in Chapter 6.

For instance, let's suppose that you want to link the series *basketball, moose, clarinet, etc.*, to the item in peg two. Let's suppose that you also wish to link *stockings, diskette, lemon, frog* to the item in peg five. The following shows the structure of these examples.

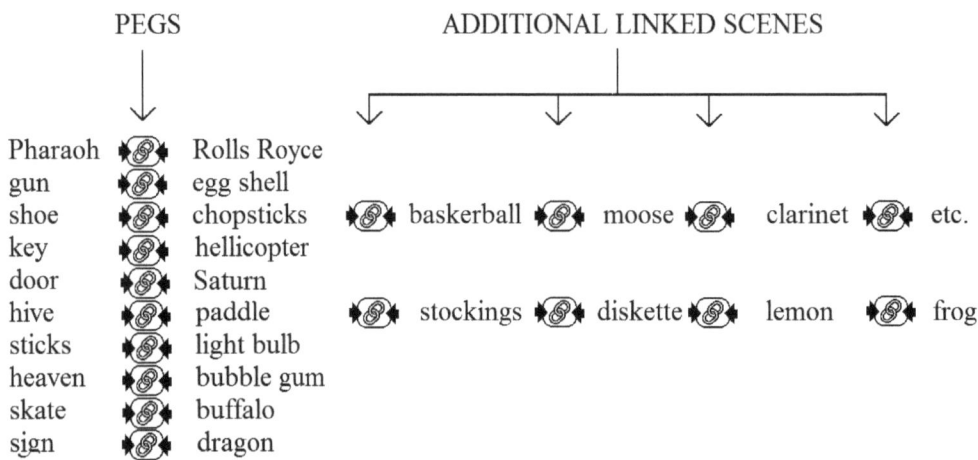

Notice the linking scene symbols, which are actually the imaginary scenes. As you may see, each mental scene connects or associates the items on both of its sides. For instance in peg two, there is a scene of shoe with chopsticks. From that scene, you form another scene of chopsticks with basketball. From this new scene, you form another scene of basketball with moose, and so forth.

Of course you can link from all the other pegs as well. In addition, this technique you can use on all the peg systems in the book. There are many examples of the use of Linking From Pegs throughout this book.

MULTIPLE BRANCHING

As I said, you can have more than just two items interacting together in a mental scene. For instance, suppose that for some reason you want to form a scene that combines *tree, rope, snowmobile,* and *floor sander.* To form this scene, you can imagine a *tree* driving a *snowmobile,* being chased by a *floor sander* that is trying to catch it using a *rope* lasso. Of course, this is just an example of a scene combining these objects. There are many other possibilities.

Such a scene can connect to more than two others. To accomplish this, one or more of the items in a scene can lead to its own next scene. Take for instance the scene above. Let's suppose that I want the *snowmobile* to lead to another scene that contains a *parrot.* To create this new scene, I could imagine a flock of parrots driving snowmobiles. Lets suppose that I now want the *tree* to lead to another scene that consists of an *office desk.* To form this scene, I could imagine such a tree sitting and working at an office desk. Now lets suppose that I want the *parrot* to lead to a scene of a *bowling ball* and *scissors.* For this, I could imagine such parrots along with scissors bowling together in a bowling alley.

The following is a diagram of these examples:

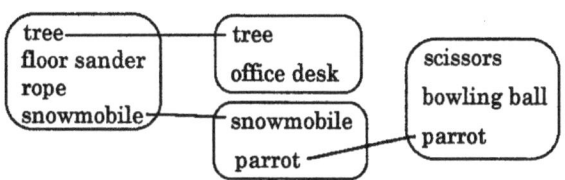

The four boxes depict mental scenes. These scenes are those I've just described. As you can see I've connected like items that lead to each other using straight lines.

Of course the number of different configurations possible using this method is infinite. Such a structure can consist of as many scenes as you want and the scenes can connect in many different ways.For recall, you can start from the very first scene then branch off into any of the others connected to it. Of a large structure of this sort, you could take many different routes.

Make a comparison of this technique to the *Links From Pegs* technique to see their similarities. The most popular name for this technique is *Mind Mapping.* As you will see in later chapters, it has many applications.

For an example of an application, you could use Multiple Branching (on page 31) to memorize an organizational structure such as the following:

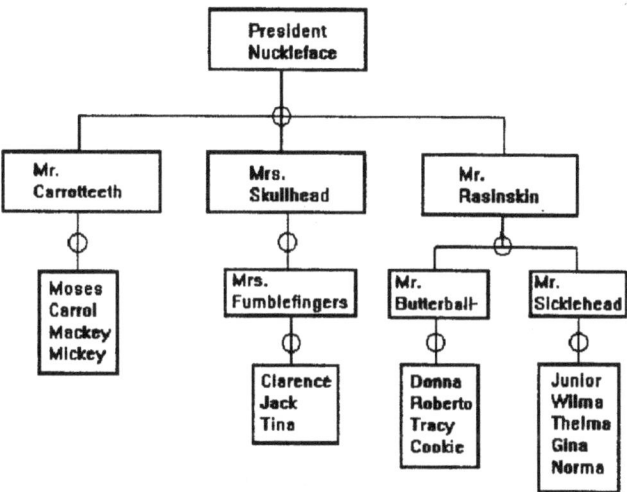

As you can see, this is a chart of some sort of chain of command structure. A person who knows all of these people could easily memorize the entire chart with the use of Multiple Branching. Of course the example above is a small chart. Never-the-less, the technique works just as well on charts much more vast and complex. I now leave it to you to figure out how to apply the technique to memorizing it. One hint is to think of the circles in the chart as mental scenes consisting of the persons attached to them.

Let's supposed that you have created the appropriate scenes to memorize the chart above. Your next question is of course, "How do I use the scenes I've just memorized?". To answer this, I will use the following examples:

Suppose that you want to recall the list of people who work under Mr. Sicklehead. First you recall any one of the scenes of Mr. Sicklehead. Then you can recall the other scenes that consist of him. Since you are the one who created the mental scenes, you would automatically know the relation of each person in such a scene. Therefore, you could determine the people working under him. In this way, you can also determine the person working over him.

Suppose that you wish to recall all the people working under Mr. Rasinskin. For this, you would begin by recalling one of the scenes of Mr. Rasinskin. Then, if you are not already thinking of it, you would recall the scene of him and his boss. From this scene, you recall the scene of Mr. Rasinskin and his subordinates. Then one after another, from this scene, you recall each scene of these two subordinates. Then you do likewise for each of Mr. Rasinskin's subordinates, and so forth.

If you ever have a task requiring you to recall a large structure of this sort, you can reconstruct the chart on paper as you recall its details.

CHAPTER 8

THE LOCI SYSTEM

In this system, one associates imaginary images with real objects. One can make this system a peg system, as we shall see.

To explain this system, I will describe how you can use the stationary items in your home to form a number peg system. To make such a system, you simply assign peg numbers to the furniture and stationary items in your home. One easy way of doing this is to move, let's say, counter clockwise around the first room you enter when entering your home. As you move, you assign numbers to, let's say, ten items or items of furniture you encounter. You then enter the next room to assign ten more numbers to increase your set, and so on. Of course, you can also select such items as your doors, walls, closets, windows, ceiling lights, wall switches, and driveway.

Let's suppose that you do proceed counter clockwise in the first room of your home, and the order of furniture and items you do encounter is: a coat rack, a large plant, a sofa, an end table, and so on. Therefore, to apply this system, you would assign peg number 0 to the coat rack. The peg number assigned to the plant next to it is 1. The sofa next to the plant is assigned peg 2, and so forth. You must also memorize the number assignment of each item.

To help you to memorize the number assignment of each stationary household item, you can use the same idea as that described on page 28 for memorizing a custom peg set. Therefore, you could associate each household item with something that reminds you of its assigned number. For example, I might imagine the coat rack playing with a hula hoop (A hula hoop shapes like a zero). Likewise, I would imagine the plant interacting with something that reminds me of the number 1, and so forth.

Let's suppose that you want to use these pegs to memorize a list. To explain this, I will use the very same list of random items on page 21 in Chapter 6, used to explain the basic number peg system. You would therefore associate Rolls Royce with that coat rack. For this, you could imagine for example, that that coat rack is there driving a small Rolls Royce in a continuous circle. Then you would associate egg shell with the plant. For example, you could apply it by imagining what it would be like if that plant were using a broom to chase away a group of smelly egg shells that are trying to climb into its flower pot. You would then associate chop sticks with the sofa, and so on. To recall any data from these pegs, you simply explore the rooms of your home mentally, which you could do at any time and place.

This system, as we have just applied it, is often called *The Roman Room System.* It is written that the ancient Romans used it for such applications as speeches, and that such a speech sometimes lasted for hours. It probably worked well for this, considering that the thoughts of ones own home can help one to relax when speaking to a crowd. I've found this system very enjoyable. Of course it requires a consistent and meticulous home arrangement. I refer to it as the Loci System because this is the name most widely used. It is a word of the ancient Romans' language. It means location, or place.

Besides a household, one can apply the Loci System to such objects as people, maps, diagrams, a figure of the human anatomy, a machine's parts, etc. For examples, a technician can use this system to memorize information about each micro-chip on a printed circuit board. A medical student can use it to memorize the names of bones on a model of a skeleton, Therefore it can be of good use in a technical or medical field. You could even apply it to piano keys, to memorize which keys to sharp or flat in order to play in a particular key. You can apply the Loci System to computer keys. For example, you could do this by associating each key's label with a mental image that depicts its programmed function. The possible applications of this system is quite vast indeed. Throughout this book, there are many examples of the use of the Loci System in such ways.

One can apply it to parts of one's own body. This can be of good use to a person who is blind or deaf. This also makes a good check list for packing clothes for a trip, and there are many other applications. In addition, it calls for the use of other senses, such as touch sensation. By assigning numbers to one's body parts, one can make this a number peg system also. Such works well for shopping lists.

One way to mentally establish such a peg system more easily is to initially place into each peg, an item that naturally reminds you of the number assignment. An example of such items are those that rhyme with numbers. Then before applying the peg set to a new list, you mentally review the pegs occasionally until you are sure you know the number assignments well. Of course, this method would also work well for the Roman Room System.

The lessons of Chapter 4 apply. To increase the effectiveness of the Loci System, think of the following phrase when applying it: "what would it be like if...". I've discovered that this phase causes the scene to seem as though it is really happening. Notice how I use this principle in the fourth paragraph of this chapter.

CHAPTER 9

THE STORY METHOD

This is another useful system to memorize a list of items in consecutive order. In most cases, you can use this instead of the *Link System*. To use this system, you form a story with the items to memorize. You are to imagine the story taking place. The lessons of Chapter 4 apply as well.

For an example, let's apply the same list on page 16, used to demonstrate the Link System. The following is such a story:

```
A dress shirt is sleeping on the bed. The alarm clock
rings which wakes up the shirt. The shirt grabs a
frying pan and throws it at the clock. The clock
catches the frying pan, then tosses it into the air.
The frying pan lands in an open dresser drawer. This
awakes a sweater that has been sleeping there. The
sweater takes the trying pan to the kitchen. There, it
uses the frying pan to fill a 6 foot tall thermos made
of linen cloth. The thermos leaks, which gets the
sweater very wet. Because it is wet, the sweater
decides that it needs ironing. The sweater then lies
on an ironing board with a strange cover. The cover is
made of stained glass. A 4 foot tall pencil sharpener
arrives and begins to dump its sharpening fragments on
the sweater. This causes the sweater to get up and
leave. The sweater returns with a can of strange motor
oil. This oil consists of millions of tiny noisy
running car engines. The sweater dumps the motor oil
on the sharpener. The sharpener goes into the bathroom
and takes a shower. The shower curtain is made of
whiskey bottles, When the sharpener is finished, it
sits down to drink a bottle of whiskey.
```

Try this with any such list. You would probably find the story easy to manifest and recall. You can also include yourself in such a story. In this case, the scenery is all around you. In addition, you could be part of the story, with you and the items interacting. There is one small disadvantage to the Story Method. It is not so easy to recall the list backwards as it is for the Link System. Nevertheless, it is possible.

CHAPTER 10

THE ALPHABET AND OTHER CHARACTERS

As you will see in later chapters, in many applications, visualizing letters is necessary. One way of doing this is to use image words that sound close to, if not exactly like, their corresponding letters. For example, one might use *ape* for A, *bee* for B, *sea* for C and so on.

I prefer to use items that resemble their corresponding letters. The following is my list:

A. an artist easel, (or metronome)
B. eyeglasses (sideways)
C. a crescent moon
D. a bow & arrow
E. a comb
F. a monkey wrench
G. A microscope
H. a ladder
I. a bone
J. a fish hook
K. a car jack
L. a boot
M. a suspension bridge
N. a roof & chimney
O. a lifesaver candy
P. a saber sword
Q. a radio dial
R. a cotter or bobby pin
S. a snake
T. a telephone pole
U. a magnet
V. an antenna
W. a tuxedo tail
X. scissors
Y. a sling shot
Z. a fire escape.

:   a traffic light
−   a shelf
×   a tire wrench
,   a gas pedal
(a plow (going from left to right)
→   an arrow (going from left to right)
±   a grave
↓   an anchor
?   a sickle
!   a bat and ball
÷   a cloths wringer

•   a raisin
+   an ambulance
=   bunk beds
↑   an umbrella
)   a shield (going from left to right)
←   a claw
;   a tide
/   a lever
'   a comet
"   tire tracks
_   a carpet

H is the 8th letter of the alphabet, just as J is the 10th. If you know the numerical place of each letter in this way, you could use the alphabet images as number pegs. One quick way to learn them is to place each alphabet image into a peg of its number. Then you could use the pegs to recall a letter's number, until you learn them. Keep this method in mind because for applications in later chapters it is quite useful.

As I've implied in one of the paragraphs on page 23, not all peg labels depict numbers. In later chapters, there are examples of the use of the items of this list as peg labels. You would find such example in systems for memorizing codes pertaining to the alphabet.

CHAPTER 11

NUMBERS

In this chapter, I will cover some ways in which the techniques can apply to memorizing numbers of a limited number of digits. In later chapters, I describe ways of memorizing numbers of many more digits.

NUMBER GROUPING

Many people memorize numbers, such as telephone numbers, by separating the digits into groups. Then they associate the groups with numbers they are familiar with, or with a pattern the combined groups appear to have.

For an example, let's suppose that you want to memorize a certain ten digit number. The first step is to look at two or more of the first digits and try to recall another number you are familiar with that is the same. For example, let's suppose that the first three digits of the number is the same as the last three digits of a phone number you frequently call. Therefore, you have just associated the first part of the number with that phone number. Let's suppose that the next two digits is the same as the last two digits of the year of your birth. Therefore, you have associated the next two digits as well.

In doing this to all the digits in the number, you would have formed a series of familiar numbers that together represent the number you want to memorize. The number is much easier to memorize in this way.

REMEMBERING IT BACKWARDS

Another aid in memorizing numbers is to learn to say the number backwards. Thus, you would memorize the number in two forms, both forwards and backwards. You could verify one form of the number with the use of it in the other form.

USING THE LINK SYSTEM

Another way of memorizing long digit numbers is to apply the Link System to item images that rhyme with, or resemble, numbers.

USING THE STORY METHOD

I've found this system very effective. To explain it, let's suppose that you wish to memorize a new girlfriend's phone number. Let's say that the number is 718-615-2894. To do it, I might imagine the following story. Again, the lessons of Chapter 4 apply.

```
The new girl is in heaven (7). Out of her pocket, she pulls
out a sugar bun (1) the bun grow legs and runs to a roller
skate (8), gets on it and begins to roll itself away. The
```

skate runs into a pile of sticks (6). The sticks begin to roll to and stuff themselves into a large cannon gun (1). The cannon fires and the sticks are propelled out hitting a bee hive (5) .The angry queen bee comes out of the hive wearing large yellow shoes (2) She then walks to a metal gate (8)and begins to kick it numerously. The noise causes a large neon sign (9) to arrive and begins to flash its light into the bee eyes to annoy it. The bee responds by pulling out an electric saw (4)turns it on and with it, she tries to cut the sign in half.

As you probably have noticed, I put the girl at the beginning of the story. The advantage of this is probably obvious. Placing this at the beginning aids in recall of the data when needed. This applies to most of the other applications in this book as well. Try this with any such number. You would most likely find that it is easy to form and recall. Also, one could include the alphabet images in such a story.

USING THE PHONETIC NUMBER CODE SYSTEM

This, I feel is the best system for memorizing numbers, and it is covered in later chapters.

CHAPTER 12

WORDS AND NAMES

For some applications, it is necessary to visualize a word whether it's an object or a term. In this chapter, my definition of a term is a word that is not the name of a person, place or physical object.

Memorization when it comes to terms can be difficult because unlike an object or noun, which you can visualize, a term normally has no image to it. Therefore, a term normally can not be visualized. On page 14, I've written about adding to certain forms of information, aspects that apply to other senses such as sight, sound, smell, etc. In this chapter, I will describe how to give a term such aspects. This involves forming a mental image of the term.

To form a mental image of a term, you must first have in mind a symbol that represents it. For instance, one way to picture the term *start,* is to picture a starting line for racing. The term *freedom* reminds me of an open cage. Therefore, I've chosen it as my image *of freedom.* For another example, my image of the term *last* is that of a caboose. A caboose is the last car of a freight train. For another example, my image for *name* is that of a name plaque or pin on name tag. This is the same principle as that of an icon, as used in computer programs and operations. Yes, in applying this to a term, you a more or less forming a mental icon of that term.

Provided it works for you, it doesn't matter what your image is for a particular term. My mental image of *thing* is that of the marvel comics fantastic four character, *the Thing.* Someone else might think instead, of the hand in the box, that is in the television comedy series: *The Adams Family.* In this show, the name of this hand is *Thing.* It is more effective to use the first image that comes to mind when you think of a particular word. Unconsciously, you have been forming images for words throughout your entire life. You are probably aware of some of them.

Another way to form a mental icon of a term is to imagine an object of which its name sounds close to the term in question. Note the following examples:

The mental icon of the term *supine* could be the image of a pine tree that drinks and spits out sap. Then you can call this sort of tree a *sap pine.* The imaginary image of the term *petrous,* because it sounds like *pet rust* could be that of a pet, such as a cat or dog, that is very rusty. The mental icon of the word *vestry* could be the image of a tree that buys and wears large colorful vests. Therefore, you call this sort of tree a vest *tree.*

As you might see by the three examples I've just given, this method is useful for a term of which you do not know the definition. Notice that of the examples, *vestry* is not a term as defined at the beginning of this chapter. A vestry is an object. I've included the word vestry to demonstrate that this method is also useful for a non-term of which you don't know the definition. Obviously, this method is useful for foreign words as well.

Another method is to separate the word into syllables, then choose the names of objects that sound similar to each. For example, the word "consciousness" sounds like "coon, chest, nest". Therefore, the image of a nest on a coon's chest would suffice.

These lessons apply to names as well because names are like terms. F or *Elliot,* it could be the image of someone sailing a yacht in an alley (alley yacht). For *Gladys* (pronounced as "gladis") the image could be that of a glass dish. For *Gloria,* the image might be that of the American flag held by a Civil War soldier. My image for this name is that of a lady's blue head scarf. Don't ask me the reason because it has been this since my childhood. I've found this last type of word image connection most effective, however, only if the image is not that of a person. In Chapter 13, I describe more about this.

Also, one could change, add or delete one or more letters in a word to change the word to an object. This should be done without changing the basic sound of the word. For example, one can change *Valenda* or *Brenda* to *blender. Brenda* could also change to *brander.*

Because one will have to apply these principles, it makes sense to form and continuously increase your list of word and name images. This would make such matters easier to handle, and less time consuming.

CHAPTER 13

PEOPLE

It is often desirable, an advantage, and even necessary, to have the ability to recall information about a person, such as, for example, his or her name. Such a skill and ability could make you quite popular and even famous. Such is probably so for the celebrities mentioned on page 7.

You may have witnessed a performance of which the performer demonstrates his or her ability to quickly recall the name of any person of the audience on sight. This performer would first learn all the names by meeting the spectators one by one while learning the name of each, before any of the spectators enter the auditorium or theater. The audience usually consisted of more than three hundred unfamiliar people. Well, In this chapter, I describe the technique or techniques this performer probably used to do it.

The most popular technique is to apply the Loci System. For this, you mentally associate a name image (such as that described in chapter 12) to the unique and most prominent and/or uncommon features of the person's face.

Therefore, to remember for instance, Mrs. Wilder's name, you might first notice, for instance, that she has big lips. Therefore, you could choose the lips as the most uncommon feature on her face. To apply this technique, you could imagine for example, how it would look, sound, and smell if a tiny welder were crawling around and working on her lips to weld them shut *(Wilder* reminds me of *welder.).*

Lets suppose that you meet a man named Mr. Samson, who has noticeably small ears. The name Samson reminds me of the strong long haired man named Samson in the bible, who, among other feats of strength, wrestled and defeated a lion. Therefore, to aid in later recalling his name, I might apply my imagination to Mr Samson's ears by imagining on them two miniatures of this strong man wrestling his ears.

For one more example, suppose that you have just met a girl named Robin Sanders, and you want to be able to recall her name should you ever meet her again. Lets suppose that her most outstanding facial feature is her long thin nostrils. For this, one could imagine that robin birds are flying around her head and sanding her nose down using miniature noisy electric sanders.

I've just now thought of the idea of connecting names to people by applying the loci system to other body parts (or applying the whole body) instead of only the head and face. I will now apply this idea to a female named Sally, as an example. For this, you could imagine her in an unforgettable situation that reminds you of her name. For example, I might imagine her kicking & turning around & over in a giant boll of salad (which sounds like the name) & dressing (in an arousing way of course ☺). For another example, If she had, for example, quite noticeable legs, I might imagine, for example, her wearing leotards made of salad & dressing.

As I've implied, this chapter, as well as the techniques taught in it, can apply to other info about people besides their names. For example, a waiter or waitress could use such techniques to aid in recalling which meal is for which customer. For another example, a coat and hat clerk could uses such techniques to help in recalling which coat belongs to which person, just in case there's ever a lost of one or more coat tickets.

CHAPTER 14

THE PHONETIC NUMBER CODE SYSTEM

This system for memorizing numbers is the most versatile and most efficient system I've seen yet. With this system, you convert numbers to words, which you then convert to the imaginary images for memorization. This chapter describes only the code itself, along with some ways of memorizing it. The next chapter describes how to use it.

The following chart is the Phonetic Code:

DIGIT	PHONETIC CODE NUMBER EQUIVALENT
0	S or Z
1	T, D, or Th
2	N
3	M
4	R
5	L
6	J, Sh, or Ch (as in chip)
7	K or G (as in goat)
8	F or V
9	B or P
BLANK	W, H, Y, vowels, or spaces

To memorize this chart, you could apply a peg system, of course. In this case, the alphabet list on page 37 can be of use. The following is a common memory aid:

- Z is for Zero
- A 1 turned 180 degrees looks somewhat like a T
- A backwards 2 turned 90 degrees looks somewhat like an N
- Turned 90 degrees, a 3 is an m, or an m is a 3.
- R is The last letter in the word FOUR.
- The five fingers, with the thumb pointed out, resemble an L
- A 6 looks almost like a backwards j
- Two 7s stuck together, of which one 7 is turned 135 degrees, looks like a K
- A lowercase F, in cursive, almost looks like an 8.
- A b turned 180 degrees, or a p backwards, looks like a 9.
- The three blank consonants spell *why*.

If you analyze these eleven statements and compare them with the chart, you probably won't have any difficulty memorizing that chart. The paragraph following this one explains other aspects of this system, that also aid in memorizing that chart. Most of the following chapters in this book will cover some applications of the Phonetic Code System. As you will now see, there are two reasons that this system is named *the Phonetic Code.*

Notice in the chart that except for the blanks, each code letter is in a group with others that sound most similar to it. For example, the sound that S makes in a word is very similar to the sound that Z makes. The only difference is that the S sound is made using more air force through the teeth. For better comprehension, for each of these ten groups, compare the sounds of its letters. If you do, you would see that such is the case with each of these groups. This is one of the reasons for the system's name. As you may have noticed, this is not the case with the Th. Nevertheless, the system must accommodate the Th. Therefore, it is put in the group with the T and D. As I've stated, these aspects will also aid in memorizing the Phonetic Code. These aspects, combined with the list of eleven statements just mentioned, provide a very strong memory aid.

Note now that in this system, words are spelled according to pronunciation. Therefore, you need not concern yourself with the usual spelling rules. This is the other reason for the system's name. Note the following examples:

> Knock would be spelled **nok**. Butter would be spelled **buter** (because for pronunciation, only one t is necessary in this word). Box would be spelled **boks**. Quick would be **kwik**. Phone would be **fone** or **foan**. Accent would be **aksent**. Action would be **akshun**. Bridge would be **brij**. Iron would be **iern**. Witch or which would be **wich**. Comb would be **koam** or **kome**. Cell or sell would be **sel**. Giant would be **jiant**, etc.

I think that covers roughly all varieties of the kind of word adaptations you might encounter. Study them well and compare. From these examples, you may have already figured out that the letters **Q, X, hard C** (as in cut), **soft C** (as in cellar), and **soft G** (as in germ) have been omitted simply because they are unnecessary. The Phonetic Code contains all the sounds needed to produce any word according to its pronunciation. In the next chapter, I provide practice on such re-spelling of words.

You would find this code very useful, so learn it and memorize it. You should learn it well before proceeding. I've read that this system is about three hundred years old. We will now progress to the next chapter that describes how to use it.

CHAPTER 15

NUMBERS WITH THE PHONETIC SYSTEM

I strongly suggest that you give this system a good chance. I say this because you may find it somewhat intimidating at first. You might even prejudge it as too much of a hassle to bother with. Also, perhaps because of the large amount of subject matter in this chapter, it might seem as if it were difficult to learn. Nevertheless, you would probably find it not so difficult to learn, well worth it, quite enjoyable, and quite handy. Therefore, don't miss out. Give it a chance. Besides, almost all of the rest of the book's contents require its use. To improve comprehension, as you go through this chapter, and when applicable, check the Phonetic Code Chart in the preceding chapter for consistency with the subject matter at hand.

As I've implied, this system provides an excellent and practical means of converting numbers to such images and scenes as those throughout this book. Basically, to use this system. You first convert the number to a series of words. Then you form imaginary scenes and images depicting the series of words. To convert the number into words, you first select a series of code letters that correspond to the number's digits. Then you insert blanks (see bottom of phonetic code chart) around and in between these letters to form the words.

For an example, let's apply the system to the new girl's phone number on page 38. Again, this number is 718 615 2894. For the first digit of this phone number (7), according to the chart on page 44, one can choose either a K or a G. For the second digit (1), it can be either a T, a D or a Th, and so on. I just want to be certain that you understand the system. Nevertheless, for this example, I will now take the liberty and choose each corresponding code letter for each digit. Let's see what happens.

Series of digits	7	1	8	6	1	5	2	8	9	4
code letters	K	T	F	Sh	D	L	N	F	B	R

As you can see, each letter I've chosen (or letter combination if it's Sh, Ch, or Th) is directly underneath its corresponding digit. For better comprehension, check each of these ten match ups for consistency with the chart on page 44.

The next step is to place blanks (see bottom of chart on page 44) around and/or in between these letters to form words. For instance, for the first two letters (K T), by placing an I in between them, and an E on the end, I can form the word KITE. I will now take the liberty and choose the blanks for the whole set. Now, by applying this principle to the entire series of letters, I've derived the following four words (For better comprehension, I've underlined the blanks.):

K<u>A</u>TF<u>I</u>SH <u>D</u>OL N<u>I</u>FE B<u>EA</u>R

As you can see, some of the spelling is incorrect. Remember from the previous chapter that the usual spelling rules do not apply in this system. Again, only pronunciation applies. Nevertheless, in the usual standard spelling, these words would have been:

catfish doll knife bear

You could easily memorize the phone number by applying this set of words to the Link System or the Story Method. To recall the number when you need it, simply extract the number from these four words. It's that simple.

To extract the number from the words, simply do the reverse process. That is, you change each letter (or letter combination if it is Th, Ch, or Sh) back to its number equivalent. Do this one by one from left to right. As you proceed, keep in mind the rule of spelling according to pronunciation. Perhaps until you become more accustomed to the system, your first step in this extraction should be to respell the words according to pronunciation.

This system is quite flexible. Had I chosen different blanks, I would have derived different words. For example, the same number also converts to *coat fish dial honey fiber.* Here, I changed only some of the blanks in the series of words above. For better comprehension, extract the number from these five words then compare the resulting number with the results from the previous series of words.

Therefore, one particular combination of code letters can provide numerous potential word combinations. Of course, most of the code letters are also changeable. This provides even more flexibility. Because of all this flexibility, one can quickly and easily apply this system to any number whatsoever.

If you wish to, you could carefully choose code letters and blanks to convert the number to a sentence. For example, the same number also converts to *Get a fish to lie on vapor.* For better comprehension, extract the number from these words then compare. Obviously, this sentence is much easier to recall than the number from which it was derived.

Practice the Phonetic Code System using pen and paper. You would probably master it very quickly. When you have mastered it using pen and paper, try doing it all mentally. The results may surprise you. From use alone, you would quickly come to know the Phonetic Code by heart. In turn, you would naturally learn to do such conversions quickly and automatically and you would never forget the system.

Again, I advise you to practice this system and give yourself a chance to become accustomed to it. You would be glad you did. To master it easily, I suggest that you form a habit of mentally applying it to all numbers you encounter, even those that you would never need to recall later.

Another effective way to use the Phonetic Code for a number is to use an acrostic. This is covered in the later chapter in this book, *miscellaneous systems.*

For a number with a decimal point, such as 145.84751, my system is to replace the decimal point with its word listed in my alphabet list on page 37 (The word for *decimal point* in that list is *raisin.*), then convert the numbers. In doing this to this number, you would derive 145 *raisin* 84751 which could then convert to *trail raisin fork light.* The number above could also converts to *Drill a raisin for gold.* This method can also apply to numbers consisting of any of the other characters in the alphabet lists on page 37.

When using this method, to avoid confusion, never convert any series of digits to any of the words (items) in either the alphabet or symbols list on page 37. For example, for the digits 514, don't convert it to *ladder,* because the word *ladder* is in one of those lists. Convert it instead to something else, such as *letter.* In this way, *ladder* can mean but one thing when applied to such an encoded number. Likewise, raisin can be but one thing. It is the decimal point and not the digits 402.

Another way of mine for dealing with decimals in numbers is to slightly change the rules of the Phonetic Code. You could for example use Th to depict the decimal point. Perhaps you could use one or more of the blank consonants (W, H, or Y) instead.

As I've stated in a previous chapter, it is helpful to connect such data to its subject. By the term *subject,* I refer to what it is the data (number) is for. For example, to memorize the phone number of the example I used, one could use the Link System and place a mental image of the girl as the first link in the series, *catfish, doll, knife, bear* (Recall this series of words from the lessons). To memorize that number, one could also imagine that the girl herself is successfully attempting to *get a fish to lie on vapor,* (Recall this sentence from the lessons.).

I have just thought of something you could do with a telephone number to increase flexibility. The addition of one or more digits to the right end of a telephone number would not affect the result when dialing it. Besides, you would probably automatically disregard such additional digits when dialing the number. This, you would do because you would know the number of digits in any telephone number. When converting a number to words (the Phonetic System), you could of course place additional letters at the end of the series. However, because of this idea when applied to telephone numbers, the additional letters do not necessarily need to be phonetic code blanks.

The following is another idea I've thought of. Besides memorization, you could use the Phonetic system to encode numbers you don't wont others to understand. For example, Let's suppose that you keep a phone book somewhere, and it becomes missing. To help prevent the finder from using the information in it, you could have all the numbers in the book encoded into words.

There are other possible applications of this idea. For instance, you could use it to form a computer or bank password which is difficult for others to figure out. Yet, the words are easy for you to memorize and derive the password from. It can be done by simply choosing a set of two or more words that remind you of what the password is for, then change it to a number (using the phonetic code). This number, you then program into the computer as the password.

To recall the password when you need to, simply recall the words and convert them to the number. It's that simple.

However, you must still be careful with the use of this code for such security matters. For example, suppose there were an unscrupulous person who is trying to figure out your passwords, who is also aware of the phonetic code, & that you use it in this way. That person would therefore learn the phonetic code then use it in the attempts to figure out your passwords. One way to deal with this problem is to modify the Phonetic code in your own secretive way. This modification could then apply only to passwords and encryption. Another method is to avoid using anything

49

that's too easy to guess. For instance, suppose that you are forming a password for your account in a bank named *Main Street Bank*. In such a case, don't use the words *main street bank*, because it's to easy to guess, then convert. However, you could use these three words securely if you add something to them that increases the passwords difficulty in guessing. For example, you could add one of more words to these three words, and the additional word or words could be something that reminds you of that particular bank (or its location, or whatever) that no-one else would think of or conjure up. For another way to increase security, it's a common practice to mix number digits with words or letters in the forming of a password. This practice, combined with using the phonetic code, provides a variety of ways to form passwords that are easy for the maker to memorize, yet impossible for anyone else to guess. Nevertheless, I leave it to you derive other such security ideas and possibilities.

The following are exercises to assure you of your comprehension of the Phonetic System. The answers are on page 163. The list of Chapter 16 on page 51 contains good examples, so give it a look.

I. Convert the following words to their phonetic code number equivalents.

1. Creation
2. gentlemen
3. barrier
4. spring
5. xylophone
6. wrestle
7. extraction
8. knowledge
9. emergency
10. disgrace
11. psychological
12. Frankenstein
13. jurisdiction
14. reconnaissance
15. mattress
16. acceleration

17. decision
18. decipher
19. information
20. ocean
21. refrigeration
22. schedule
23. scientific
24. anchor
25. choreography
26. Christmas
27. chiropractor
28. financial
29. ballet
30. theater
31. Manhattan
32. champagne

33. a tree grows in Brooklyn
34. never give a sucker an even break
35. happiness is but a state of mind
36. 1 heard it through the grape vine
37. opportunity is often disguised as hard work
38. don't bite the hand that feeds you

II. Match each number on the left with its word equivalent on the right.

1. 147014
2. 750
3. 17014
4. 395
5. 0584
6. 41
7. 7500
8. 795
9. 1727
10. 14
11. 0747
12. 3495
13. 017270
14. 0584
15. 14014
16. 7500
17. 147014
18. 0741
19. 14
20. 017270

A. water
B. cable
C. maple
D. earth
E. dog star
F. throw
G. texture
H. techniques
I. eyeglasses
J. dragster
K. silver
L. glass
M. employee
N. mobile
O. table
P. marble
Q. table
R. couple
S. stockings
T. drugstore

CHAPTER 16

THE PHONETIC SYSTEM AS A PEG SYSTEM

In my opinion, the Phonetic code is very good for forming a peg set. The list below consists of examples of peg labels from 0 to 99. As you can see, each of the words in the list converts to its corresponding number by the Phonetic Code. Of course, one could easily extend this list. For example, 100 could be daisies, 101 could be toast, and so on. Also, one can change many of the labels to suit one's self. You can even combine words to extend the list. For instance, you could use *oily cherry* to depict 564, and *hot iron* to depict 142, etc.

There are three words I've thought of that do not convert to any number. They are, *hay*, *Hawaii* and *yoyo*. Therefore any one of these three words can be used as blanks.

0. house
1. tie
2. honey
3. ham
4. hair
5. oil
6. witch
7. key
8. hoof
9. whip
10. toes
11. tooth
12. tin
13. tomb
14. tire
15. tool
16. dish
17. tack
18. dove
19. tuba
20. nose
21. wand
22. nun
23. Nemo
24. wiener
25. nail

. hay
26. notch
27. neck
28. knife
29. knob
30. mouse
31. meat
32. woman
33. mummy
34. hammer
35. mule
36. match
37. hammock
38. movie
39. Wimby
40. rose
41. road
42. iron
43. rum
44. rower
45. rail
46. roach
47. rock
48. roof
49. harp
50. lace

Hawaii
51. wallet
52. lion
53. lamb
54. lyre
55. lily
56. leash
57. log
58. olive
59. lip
60. cheese
61. sheet
62. chain
63. chime
64. cherry
65. jail
66. judge
67. shake
68. chef
69. ship
70. hacksaw
71. coyote
72. wagon
73. gum
74. car
75. clay

. yoyo
76. cage
77. cake
78. cave
79. cage
80. fuse
81. foot
82. phone
83. foam
84. fire
85. fly
86. fish
87. fig
88. viva
89. fab
90. bus
91. boat
92. piano
93. bomb
94. bear
95. beef
96. peach
97. bike
98. beef
99. popeye

To help memorize this set, I used the *forming a custom peg set* method as described on page 28 (the rhyming list). Of each of the 100 pegs (scenes) above, I've added to the peg (scene), that particular item of the rhyming list that depicts the right most digit of that peg number.

For example, for peg 94, I formed a scene of *bear*s in a zoo. Then to help in memorizing the number assignment of this peg (scene), I took the right most digit of 94, which is 4, then placed into this peg (scene), the item of the rhyming list, door (for four). For this, I imagined the *bear*s in that scene continuously walking upright while opening then walking through, then closing and slamming a maze of *door*s in their zoo cage. For another example, for peg 52 (lion), I imagine the *lion*s in their zoo cage wearing tap *shoe*s while tap dancing, sometimes using all four of their legs and paws, and sometimes while standing walking upright.

Then before applying the peg set to a new list, I sometimes practiced recalling the pegs until I was satisfied that I knew all the pegs and peg labels well enough. If I had any difficulty recalling a peg of a particular number, I would think of items that convert to that number as I think of the item that rhymes with the leftmost digit.

Here's an example: Suppose that I had difficulty recalling the scene that is peg 94. For this, I would think of the names of items that convert to 94 by the Phonetic code, such as pear, berry, bear, boar, beer, pier, etc. I would also think of phonetic code pegs in which I placed a *door* (rhymes with four). Of course, one of these phonetic code words would bring to mind the peg containing both doors and bears. Thus, it brings to mind the proper peg.

A person who has been using the phonetic code very much would find this method very helpful.

CHAPTER 17

THE WEEKLY SCHEDULE

This is an example of a system one can construct. Again, I use the Phonetic System. I also use the Multiple Branching method as taught on page 31. As you study it, I suggest that you draw diagrams for better comprehension.

Before I start, I must state five rules.

First, I form seven pegs of which each peg label depicts a different day of the week. In the lessons here, I use phonetic code number peg labels. However, it isn't necessary to use phonetic code peg labels. you could use peg labels of which each is an image that represents one of the seven weekdays. You may find this easier to use.

If you use phonetic code peg labels, never use such names to label any other pegs, and I don't use them to convert the first digit of any number. I prefer to consider Sunday as day 0. The following are the labels:

Sunday is *zoo* (0)
Monday is *toy* (1)   Tuesday is *Noah* (2)
Wednesday is *yam* (3) Thursday is *rye* (4)
Friday is *owl* (5)   Saturday is *watch* (6)

Second, the time of day is in a one, two or three digit format. The first one or two digits depict the hour and the following (last) digit, if any, depicts the minute past the hour.

Third, the first digit depicts the hours from 1 to 9. However, the hours 10, 11 and 12, convert to 00, 01 and 02 respectively.

Forth, I round off the minute past the hour to its nearest quarter hour. For 0 to 14 minutes past the hour, I omit the last digit. For 15 to 29 minutes past, the last digit is a 2. For 30 to 44 minutes, it's a 3. For 45 to 59, I use a 4. Personally, I prefer not to use a 0 nor a 1 in this case.

Fifth, To indicate A.M. I insert bright light into the scene. For P.M., I simply omit it.

The following are examples of time codes:

11:00 is 01	9:04 is 9	9:45 is 94	10:45 is 004
10:03 is 00	9:00 is 9	1:53 is 14	12.25 is 022

Let's suppose That I want to memorize the following schedule:

- The dentist at 8:00 A.M. on Tuesday

- The car mechanic at 4:20 P.M. on Wednesday

- A job interview at 11:33 A.M. on Wednesday, at 124 Church St.

- Tape the ball game on channel 7, at 4:47 P.M. on Sunday

For the first appointment, I place dentist in the peg labeled Noah. I then link from dentist, the time code, which is hoof (8). Then I see another scene of a dentist working on a patient with a hoof for one of his feet. With it, the patient kicks the dentist who is shining a bright light into his face.

I see a dentist working on the animals in Noah's ark. Then I see another scene of a dentist working on a patient with a hoof for one of his feet. With it, the patient kicks the dentist who is shining bright light into his face.

For the second appointment, I place *car mechanic* in the peg labeled **yam.** I then link from *car mechanic,* the time code, which is *rhino* (42). Addition information would then be linked to *rhino.* For example, I might imagine the following:

I see a huge orange yam as it works on a car in a town inhabited by yams. The yams surely smell good. Then I see another scene in which a car mechanic is working on a noisy rhino. The mechanic's manner in much the same as that of the yam.

For the third appointment, I must place *job interview* in the peg **yam** with *car mechanic*. I might imagine the following:

I see that the yam is still working on the car. However, it's now also wearing a suit and giving another yam a job interview as well. Then I see another scene in an office where a giant green stem (013) is wearing the same suit. The stem is giving a job interview to another stem. It is also shining a bright light in the other stems face. They both smell like stems and the light is making a weird sound. Then I see a scene of a giant stem driving a church down a street. The stem is throwing paint thinner (124) which splashes in my face.

For the forth appointment, I also need the precise minutes, to set the VCR I might imagine the following:

I see smelly zoo animals playing ball in an enormous zoo cage. They are making grunting and roaring sounds, as they usually do. Then I see a scene of ball players playing ball in a stadium in much the same way the animals were. The same animals are now the spectators. The ball players are using a man rowing a boat (rower for 44) as their ball. Then I see another scene of a giant key *(7)* sitting on a television set, that continuously changes channels as it floats in a lake. The key is rowing it as if it were a boat. Then I see a scene of keys having a rock (47 minutes) fight with clocks

The following is a diagram of these examples:

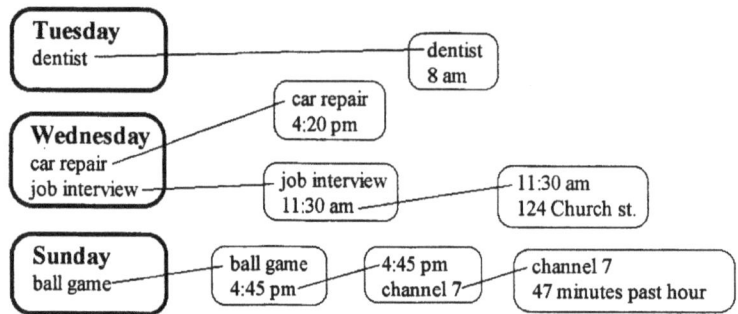

Compare this diagram to that on page 31 used in explaining the *Multiple Branching* method. Again, the boxes depict the imaginary scenes. However, instead of the actual items to imagine, I inserted into the boxes above, the information the items depict. For better comprehension, I've thickened the boxes of the day of the week pegs. Now, had I inserted the items instead, I would have created a diagram somewhat like the following:

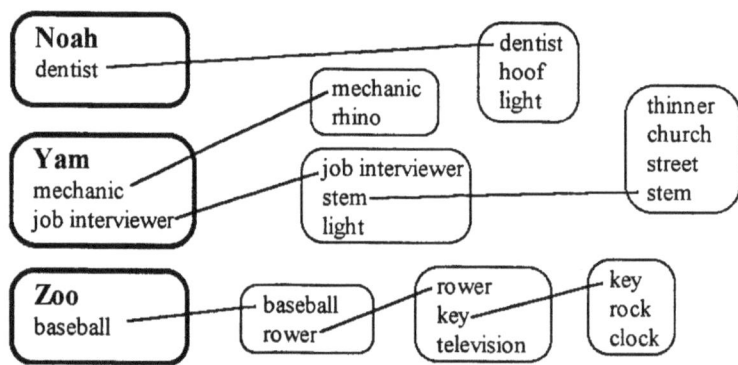

Perhaps it is more feasible for you to draw such diagrams then apply the memory technique to memorizing it. To recall the schedule of a particular day, simply review the pegs and links of that day. It make sense to review all of them regularly. Of course, one can change the system to suit one's self.

For better comprehension of the subject matter of this chapter, I want you th do the following exercise:

Review this chapter. Mentally form all the scenes described. Close the book, then recall the imaginary scenes the recall all the information about the schedule.

CHAPTER 18

THE YEARLY SCHEDULE

This is another example of a system you could design. This system is quite similar to that of Chapter 17. To comprehend this system, you must know some aspects of the system of that chapter.

Again, I use the Multiple Branching and the Linking from Pegs Techniques. The pegs depict the date numbers. Therefore, the system consists of 31 pegs, each for a monthly date. From each peg, I place the months in which there are appointments on days of that particular date number. From each of these months, I form a linking scene containing the time of the appointment. From each time indication. I create a linking scene that contains the event, and so on. To show the rest of the details and for better comprehension, I've included the following diagram:

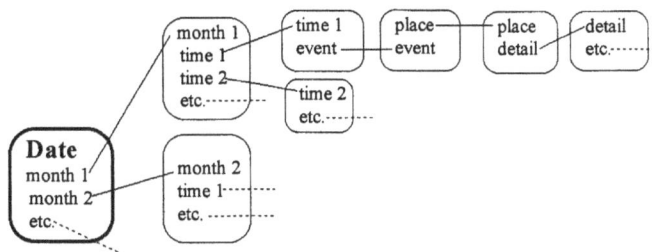

As in the previous chapter, I've thickened the boxes of the pegs. However, in this particular diagram there is but one peg. Notice that the six scenes at the top are linked together such as of the *Links From Pegs* technique. Notice also the two scenes on the bottom and at what point they connect to those above.

Now let's suppose that you want to use this system to memorize the following schedule:
- A lunch date at 42 16th Ave. 2:15 P.M. on Jan. 15
- A birthday party at 119 33 225th St. at 9:00 P.M. on May 15, of which you are required to bring a gift.
- A job test at 43 Chambers St. 11:32 A.M. on Nov. 15
- A dinner date to pick up at 543 Nicholas Blvd. at 8:00 P.M. on May 17.
- A school performance at 8:00 A.M. on May 15

Of course you don't have to apply all of the appointments and details at once. Besides, if this were the case, the system would be impractical. Nevertheless, before adding an appointment to the system, you should plan and organize its details.

To apply the examples above you could organize the system to the details as follows:

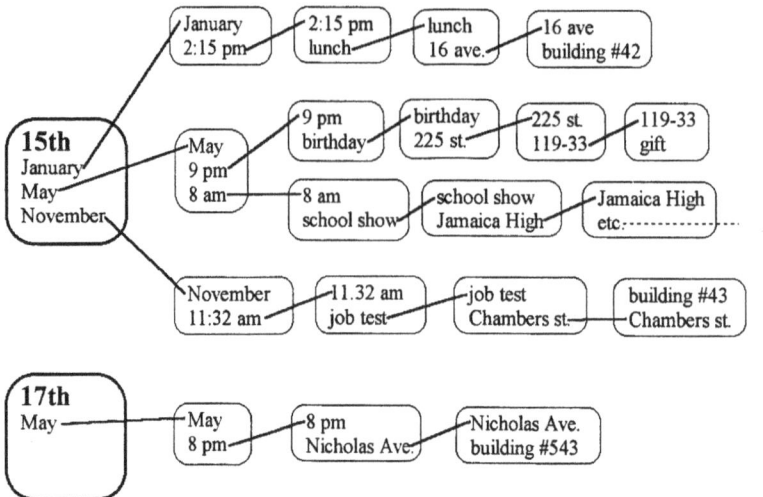

Now compare this diagram with the previous one. Again, I did not place the actual images into the scenes. I placed into them instead the data each image depicts. At this point in the book, I am sure that you know how to replace such data with the actual images. I now leave it to you to experiment with this system.

CHAPTER 19

DAYS OF DATES

There are times when it is convenient if you can quickly derive the weekday a date falls on. It is also an impressive stunt. I will cover two systems. The first system covered is one for dates within a particular year. The second one is for any date within a century.

> At this point, I must state that throughout this chapter, the word *day* depicts one of the seven weekdays (Sunday, Monday, Tuesday, etc.). Don't mistake it for *date*.

FOR THE YEAR

Provided one knows the day before the first day of the month, one can derive the day of the date in question. This could be done by simply counting the dates along with their corresponding days. One begins with the first, until one reaches the date in question. Its corresponding day would be the answer. It's simple logic.

You could make this process quicker by counting in sevens until you are close to the date in question. This is logical since the 7th, the 14th, the 21st and the 28th day would be the same day as the day before the 1st. To better understand this, look at any standard wall calendar to verify that this is so. Therefore, you would simply choose the highest of the five dates I've just mentioned, which are 0, 7, 14, 21, & 28 (Notice that the date of the very day before the first of the month is counted as 0.). Also, the date chosen of the five must be yet lower than the date in question. Then you could begin counting from the chosen date along with its corresponding day.

For an example, take the calendar on this page. In this calendar, the day before the 1st is of course a Tuesday (Remember that that date I counted as 0.). As you can see, the dates directly below this date are of the same dates as those listed in the previous paragraph. As I've said, this is so in all calendars of this format. I will now show how to use these aspects to quickly derive the day of a particular date. Let's suppose that you don't have this calendar at hand to look at. Also, let's suppose however that you do know that the day before the first is a Tuesday. Now suppose that you want to derive the day that the 24th falls on. For this, you simply chose **21** (The highest of the five dates that is yet lower than the 24th.) which is of course on a Tuesday as well. Since the 21st is on a Tuesday, the 22nd is on a Wednesday. In turn, the 23rd is on a Thursday and **the 24th is on a Friday**. Thus, I can easily find the answer, and it can easily be done mentally.

			MAY			
S	M	T	W	T	F	S
			1	2	3	4
5	6	7	8	9	10	11
12	13	14	15	16	17	18
19	20	21	22	23	24	25
26	27	28	29	30	31	

Now compare this procedure with the calendar above. If you do, you would see that this procedure in view of that calendar is like beginning at date 0, moving three steps down, then moving three steps to the right.

As for applying this principle to a whole year, you simply memorize the days before the first, in their order, for the whole year. This could be done, of course, with the use of the Peg System. Another way is to memorize a twelve number series, of which the numbers correspond to these days.

For an example, for the year 2015, you can memorize the days before the first by memorizing the following series:

| 3 | 3 | 6 | 2 | 4 | 0 | 2 | 5 | 1 | 3 | 6 | 1 |

Each digit is for one of the months of the year. As in the Weekly Schedule System on page 53, I consider Sunday as 0, Monday as 1, Tuesday as 2, etc. Therefore, the first or leftmost digit is for January, and since the number in it is 1, the series shows Monday as the day before the first day in January. The second digit is for February, and the 4 in it depicts the day before the first of that month as Thursday, and so on. Of course, one can easily derive such a number series from examining any calendar for a particular year.

Each number in the series above is but one digit. Therefore, you could turn the series into a twelve digit number simply by removing the cells around them then decreasing the spaces between the numbers. This would of course result in the following: Then you can apply a memory technique to memorizing this twelve digit number.

336240251361

To aid in finding a particular digit in this number quickly, separate the digits into four groups of three, such as follows:

336   240   251   361

Then convert each of these four groups to an imaginary item using the Phonetic Code. For the number just mentioned, the imaginary items could be:

mummy shoe,   wine rose,   nail tea,   match tie.

Yes, imagine, for example what a mummy shoe would be like. Imagine, for example, a rose that smells and tastes like wine, and quickly melts in the mouth to become wine. Imagine what nail tea would be like. etc.

For an example, to quickly derive the day that September the 18th falls on. First, as you probably already know, September is the 9th month. Then by doing some quick simple mental counting (123, 456, 789, ...) you would quickly derive that that the 9th digit is the last digit within the third group of numbers. Therefore it is of the words *nail tea*. Converting *nail tea* to a number I derive 251. Since the last digit of this number is 1, the day before the first is a Monday. Then mentally going down the calendar (7. 14. 21. 28) to the Monday before the 18th (which is 14 of course), Then by mentally counting in days to the 18th, (15, 16, 17, 18) while also thinking of the corresponding days (Tuesday, Wednesday, Thursday, Friday, I derive Friday as the answer. It's that simple.

For even more speed, remember that the first letters of each of the four words are for January, April, July and October respectively. To memorize this, you can use some sort of mnemonics, such as an acronym or acrostic.

For the year 1992, the number to memorize is 256240251361. For the year 1994, the number is 511462403513. For the year 1995, it is 622503514624. For the year 1996, it is 034025036146. For the year 1998, it is 366240251361. For the year 2000 it is 623614625035, For the year 2005, it is 511462403513 (the same as that of 1994) and so on. Again, you can easily derive such a number by observing a calendar of the year in question. As you observe, you of course list the days before the first of the months, then convert this list to digits as depicted in the lessons.

To comprehend the next system, it is important to know this system well.

FOR THE CENTURY

I include this system because I have seen it demonstrated on television in an advertisement for another memory course. I would bet that someone who reads this book will want to be able to do it. I cannot think of any use for this system other than as a stunt. For example,

given the month, date, and year, you could quickly determine which day of the week is that of a certain person's birth. Perhaps you can think of other uses, such as in the field of astrology. Nevertheless, it is an excellent way to practice the techniques and to develop the mind. On second thought, a lawyer cross examining a person in court could quickly determine the day of a date and year in question. It could also help a person to catch another in a deception. For instance, in some cases, one could tell whether another had truly engaged in a particular activity, or been to a particular place on a day in question.

Because I explain this system in depth, the lesson is very long. Also, the lesson is long because I believe in explaining some things in more than one way, to assure comprehension. Do not assume that this system is difficult to learn simply because the lesson is long. Never let the length of a lesson discourage you. I do admit that I may have explained it in more detail than necessary. I do want you to fully understand all the concepts of its making. I first explain the system in great depth, then on page 65, I summarize the entire procedure. I recommend that you first skim through it quickly, then review it in depth.

Many of the procedures used in this system are from the previous one. One must learn that system first. I must state that this system would take a little more time and practice to master. Nevertheless, don't be foolish by letting this discourage you. Try it and judge for yourself.

Before I begin to explain the system, I will now explain about the leap year, and how to find the most recent leap year before a year in question. I think that it is helpful and in many ways necessary to have a good understanding and knowledge of this in order to use the system effectively.

These next three paragraphs explain the Leap Year. The purpose of the leap year is to synchronize the calendars with a set number of complete earth rotations. Actually, there is always an extra 1/4 rotation at the end of each trip around the sun (a year). The reason is that the speed at which the Earth spins on its axis is slightly higher than the perfect speed. Therefore, the Earth completes 365 rotations (days) slightly before (6 hours before) it completes its orbit around the sun. Then in the remaining 6 hours of the orbit it rotates an extra ¼ rotation. This would eventually cause an inconsistency of the calendar with the times of the seasons if it were not compensated for.

The leap year compensates for this. The only difference between a leap year and a non leap year is that a February during a leap year has 29 days instead of 28. Beginning with the very first year of a century, leap years occur each 4 years. Therefore, the years 1900, 1904, and 1908 are examples of leap years. In summary, adding a day to the calendar each 4 years compensates for the extra 1/4 rotation each year.

I must admit now that the true time period of the earth's orbit is not 365 days and 6 hours. It is 365 days, 5 hours, 48 minutes, and 46 seconds, which is close. Because of this, there is more to the leap year system than stated here. Nevertheless, for our purpose, what I've given is good enough.

In this system, one must find the most recent leap year before a year in question. These next seven paragraphs pertain to this. As you may already see, there are very easy and logical patterns to follow to determine quickly whether a year is a leap year. Also, because of such patterns, one can easily find the most recent leap year before a particular year. I suggest that you try to derive one or more such patterns on your own before continuing. This would enhance your comprehension of this subject matter. Use some of the information I've already given.

For one pattern, for any century, years ending with **00, 20, 40, 60**, and **80** are leap years. For any of these five years, adding **4**, **8**, **12** or **16** results in the last two numbers of another leap year. It's very simple arithmetic. For instance, to find the most recent leap year before the year 1938, you could simply choose the most resent year of the five above (00, 20, 40, 60, and 80) which is of course 20. Then you add 16 to derive 36. It is easy to add 16 by merely increasing the first digit by 1 then making the last digit a 6.

Study the following scale, which I've made for better comprehension of the entire concept:

This scale shows in their relative positions, the numbers I've just mentioned. This scale is a chart of the last two of all the leap years of any century. Therefore, each vertical mark on the line is for a certain leap year. Some marks I've left blank, and I know that you can figure out what number belongs on each. To improve your understanding of this subject matter, I suggest that you do this for each and every mark on that scale. From doing this, you would see a pattern in the numbers, which is exactly what I want you to see. You should analyze the scale above and learn the pattern well.

Of course, every non leap year is somewhere in between any two bordering marks, along with two other consecutive non leap years. For instance, between the leap years 1944 and 1948, the non leap years are 1945, 1946, and 1947.

What it is you must learn to do is to quickly determine which two consecutive leap years the year in question is in between. Then the most recent leap year is of course the earlier of the two. For an example, let's find the most recent leap year before the year 1957. If you know the pattern well, you would immediately see that that year is somewhere in between the leap years 1956 and 1960. From this, you would automatically know that the most recent leap year is the earlier, which is 1956.

I advise that you practice this because you will have to use it. Try it a few times. To check the answer, simply divide the result by 4. If the result is the last two of a leap year, it would divide evenly. To check the answer, you can also use the scale on page 61. When checking an answer, if the number you had derived is the last two of a leap year, it has a mark on that scale.

To begin, you must memorize a corresponding day to each of the twelve months. For this, you could of course use the system of which you memorize a twelve digit number, as explained on page 59. In this case, the number to memorize is the number below this paragraph. As in the previous date system, each number depicts the day before the first of the month, for a whole year.

0 3 3 6 1 4 6 2 5 0 3 5

However, instead of using that method, I prefer to use 12 pegs for this. I find the use of such pegs to be a quicker. Of course each peg label depicts a particular month and I place one such weekday into each peg. Therefore, the pegs would be as follows:

PEG LABELS	PEGS	PEG CONTENTS
January	🔘	Sunday
February	🔘	Wednesday
March	🔘	Wednesday
April	🔘	Saturday
May	🔘	Monday
June	🔘	Thursday
July	🔘	Saturday
August	🔘	Tuesday
September	🔘	Friday
October	🔘	Sunday
November	🔘	Wednesday
December	🔘	Friday

Of course, one must derive mental images for the elements of each peg. For instance, for the peg at the top of the list, one must have an image to depict January, and an image to depict Sunday. Since I've already explained the basic peg system as well as Words and Names (see page 40), I need not go into any more detail about this. Let's call these pegs **The Standard Month Pegs**. As you will see, you find the correct day before the first of a month for a particular year by advancing the day found in that peg a certain number of steps. Such steps is a number found in another peg set that I will describe later.

You do not need to know or concern yourself with the contents the next two paragraphs. Nevertheless, I include them for interested readers. For better comprehension, I suggest that you do skip these two paragraphs now, then return to them when you have learned the rest of the subject matter well.

For leap years, a slight modification is necessary. The modification is that for January and February during a leap year, the day found is also to be moved back one step. All of this is explained later. If it were not for the extra day in a leap year, such a modification would not be necessary. Also, finding the day of a date would be much simpler. In addition, there would be no need for such a steps peg set as that I've just mentioned. You would be able to derive the correct number of steps for a particular year using simple mathematics alone. The correspondence of days to dates would shift at a simple linear rate for all years. That is, for every date in a new year, its corresponding weekday would be the weekday after that of the same date of the previous year. However the shift rate is not so simple as this. One must also consider that there are two shiftings during a leap year. One such shifting, like all other years, is at the beginning of the year. The other is at the day after February. Since leap years occur every four years, the simple linear rate I've described is offset every four years.

Each *steps number* in the peg set I will soon describe has been pre-modified to make it easier to compensate for this shift problem. The pre-modification is that each *steps number* in each peg has been increased by one. However, if the number is six, it has been decrease by six (changed to zero) instead. The advantage of this pre-modification is that one would only have to compensate for a January or February during a leap year. Without this advantage, one would have to compensate for all other dates, thus making such a compensation necessary much more frequently.

The next step is to memorize a set of numbers of which each number corresponds to a different leap year of a century. The following is a list of the last two digits of the leap years of the 20th century, with their corresponding numbers:

00 -0	20 -4	40 -1	60 -5	80 -2
04 -5	24 -2	44 -6	64 -3	84 -0
08 -3	28 -0	48 -4	68 -1	88 -5
12 -1	32 -5	52 -2	72 -6	92 -3
16 -6	36 -3	56 -0	76 -4	96 -1

There are 25. Of course, you can use 25 pegs for this, and I've found this easiest to work with. For those who decide to memorize them in this way, the following is but a suggestion:

Use the Phonetic Code pegs on page 51 for the leap years (peg labels), and use item images of one of the peg lists in Chapter 6 on page 20 for the number to be placed into each peg. Of the list above, let's call such pegs the **leap year pegs** and let's call the corresponding number to each leap year a **steps number**.

For an example of such a peg, for the year 1900, one could imagine that the pharaoh *(steps number* is 0) is trying to sleep in a tent size house (Phonetic Code peg 00) made of calendars. Since he uses nothing to fasten them together, the house continuously collapses or blows away. This causes him embarrassment in the presence of his subjects. Nevertheless, he continuously rebuilds it himself, and he won't take any advice. For another example, you could imagine a scene in a field in which giant grains of rice (Phonetic Code peg 40) are having a gun fight *(steps number* is 1). Instead of smoke, calendars float from the barrels of the guns. Notice that of each example, I've included the element of a calendar.

Another way is to use 5 pegs with 5 digits in each. The following are the pegs and *steps numbers* for the 20th century:

0	05316	20	42053	40	16420
60	53164	80	20531		

Each digit of any of the five digit numbers above depicts a *steps number*. One could memorize these numbers and match-ups using the Phonetic Code as follows:

0	slimmed shoe	20	horn salami	40	dish rinse
60	lamb teacher	80	nasal meat		

Peg 0 contains the *steps numbers* for 1900, 1904, 1908, 1912 and 1916 respectively. Peg 20 contains those for 1920, 1924, 1928, 1932 and 1936, etc.

For example, you could imagine that you are in a butcher shop for special meats. Instead of eating this type, you are to sniff it (nasal meat). This meat is more enjoyable if sniffed while placed into electrical fuses (peg 80) of which the fuse box resembles a calendar. For another example, where one buys salami, there is a special type of salami. It has the shape of a horn (horn salami). You can find out the present date just by blowing it like a horn. However, only when using your nose (peg 20) instead of your mouth.

For the 21st century, they are the following:

0 - 64205	20 - 31642	40 - 05316
60 - 42053	80 - 16420	

As you may notice, there is a 7 digit pattern that continues into the next century. Also, notice that each steps number is one less than the corresponding 20th century number. Therefore, to find the day of a date that is in the 21st century, simply perform all the procedures as if the date is of the 20th century. Then move the final result back a day. To find the day of a date in the 19th century, again perform the same procedures for 20th century dates. However, for this, you move the final result forward two days instead.

Finding the *steps number* for any non-leap year is simple. For this, first obtain from the leap year pegs the steps number of the most recent leap year before the year in question. Then count forward until you reach the year in question. As you count, increase that steps number by one each count. The result would be the correct steps number for that year.

For example, suppose that you want to find the steps number for the year 1978. In this case, the most recent leap year is 1976 and the steps number for that year is 4. Then since 1978 is two more than 1976, you increase the steps number (4) by two, resulting in 6. Therefore, the steps number for 1978 is 6

It is possible for the result of such a procedure to be a number greater than 6, and this might cause confusion for some. In this case, one could simply subtract 7 from the result. However, most of the counting for this system is done in days instead of numerals. Because days begin again on Sunday after Saturday, this subtraction wouldn't be necessary. A demonstration of this will appear in the third example, which is on page 65 near the end of this chapter.

I will now summarize the entire procedure. As you will see, the procedure is in four steps. With a little practice, a person could perform this entire procedure mentally in as little as two seconds. The steps to derive the day of a date are:
- From the Standard Month Pegs (which you are to memorize), find the corresponding day for the month in question. In the next step, consider this day to be the day before the first of the month.
- the leap year pegs (which you are to memorize) and the appropriate arithmetic, find the steps number for the year in
- question. Then move the day found in the previous step a number of paces equal to that *steps number.*
- If the month is either January or February, and the year is a leap year, consider the correct day to be the day before the one derived. Otherwise it is the correct day.

The procedure seems complicated' doesn't it? Nevertheless, with a little practice, this can be done mentally and quickly. A date is usually given in the format of month, date then year. I've designed this system with this in mind. This enables one to mentally do the calculations as one receives the date and year.

For example, to find the week-day on which June 24, 1957 fell, the steps are:
- According to the *Standard Month Pegs,* Thursday is the day to use in the next step.
- Counting corresponding days to dates, the day in the month turns out to be Sunday.
- From the *leap year pegs,* the *steps number* for the year 1956 (the most recent leap year) is 0. From 56 to 57 is but one step up. Therefore you move the *steps number* (0) one step up, making it a 1. Forwarding Sunday by 1 makes it Monday.
- Since it is not a leap year, nor is the month January or February, the answer is Monday.

For another example, to find the day of February 3, 1976, the steps are:
- According to the *Standard Month Pegs,* Wednesday is .the day to use in the next step.
- Counting corresponding days to dates, the day in the month turns out to be Saturday.
- From the *leap year pegs,* the *steps number* for 76 is 4. Forwarding Saturday 4 days changes it to Wednesday.
- The year is a leap year and the month is one of the first two. Therefore, the answer is the day before, which is Tuesday.

For another example, for April 19, 1947, the steps are:
- According to the *Standard Month Pegs,* Saturday is the day to use in the next step.
- Counting corresponding days to dates, the day in the month turns out to be Thursday.
- The most resent leap year before 1947 is 1944. From the *leap year pegs,* we find the *steps number* for 44 to be 6. Since 47 is 3 more than 44, we add 3 to the 6, changing it to 9. Moving Thursday ahead 9 days changes it to Saturday (Obviously it would actually be 2 days ahead, since 9 days is one week plus 2 days.)
- Since it isn't a leap year, nor is the month January or February, the answer is

Saturday.

For one final example, for April 19, 1972, the steps are:
- According to the Standard Month Pegs, Saturday is the day to use in the next step.
- Counting corresponding days to dates, the day in the month turns out to be Thursday.
- From leap year peg 72, the steps number is 6. Moving the days forward from Thursday, 6 steps, we arrive at Wednesday (Obviously, we would arrive at the day before Thursday.).
- The year is a leap year, However, the month is nether January nor February. Therefore, the answer is Wednesday.

There are similar systems in other books to perform the same task. With sonw thought, such a system is not difficult to create.

Some helpful tips:

- It is sometimes quicker to move a weekday backwards. For example it's quicker to move backwards by two days than it is to move forwards by five days.
- Learn to easily think of weekdays in reverse order.
- In the third step, after finding the day in the month, think of this day with the year in question. For instance, in the second step in the first example, I would think to myself, "Sunday 57".
- If at the very start you see that the date is of the first two months of a leap year, decrease the date by one (If it is the first, it becomes zero.) then omit the fourth step. In fact, I always look for such cases in the beginning, because I've often forgotten to apply the fourth step.

The following is a modification of the four steps, to make the entire calculation even easier. However, for better comprehension, I recommend that you first learn the procedure well without this modification.

What I have done here is change the third step to a more shortcut way of doing it. I've changed that step to the following:

- Decrease the year in question until it becomes the most recent leap year. As you do this, move the day in the month forward the same number by which you have decreased that year. Then move the resulting day forward a number of steps equal to the most recent leap year's *steps number*.

Applying this modification to the third example, the third step of that example changes to the following:

- To change the year in question (1947) t& the most recent leap year (1944), I must decrease it by three. Therefore, we move the day in the month (Thursday) ahead by three, thus changing it to 2-iiiday. The *steps number* of the most recent leap year is six. Therefore, I must move the Sunday forward by six (or backwards by one if you prefer this instead). Thus, it becomes Saturday.
- Using the procedure explained in the first five paragraphs of For the Year on page 59, determine the day in the month.

I now leave it to you to study this modification to se why it works.

The following are exercises for practice. The answers are on page 163.

Find the days of the following dates:

1. 09-01-64_____
2. 11-21-46_____
3. 08-21-34_____
4. 04-26-52_____
5. 01-21-58_____
6. 02-01-35_____
7. 10-16-21_____
8. 05-16-18_____
9. 05-01-27_____
10. 03-04-63_____
11. 06-28-57_____
12. 02-03-28_____
13. 02-09-19_____
14. 01-01-68_____
15. 04-08-46_____
16. 07-17-70_____
17. 09-30-40_____
18. 12-14-23_____
19. 06-18-71_____
20. 08-09-19_____
21. 11-15-06_____
22. 12-04-59_____
23. 01-01-01_____
24. 07-04-50_____
25. 02-28-60_____
26. 08-17-83_____
27. 03-17-57_____
28. 07-17-04_____
29. 12-31-75_____
30. 04-24-42_____
31. 02-28-63_____
32. 08-06-58_____

CHAPTER 20

TWO DIMENSIONAL PEGS WITH THE PHONETIC SYSTEM

Let's consider the figure below. As you probably see, it is the upper left portion of a letter/number coordinated grid.

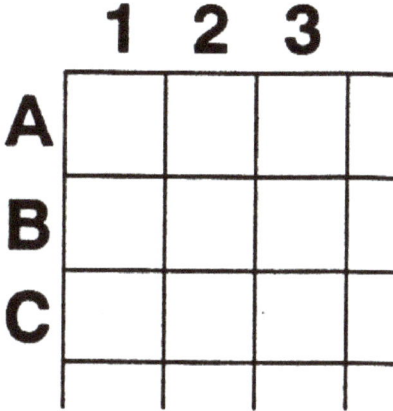

To label square C1, one could use the word *coat*. The first letter of this word depicts row C. Of the rest of the letters in this word (-oat) convert them to their phonetic code equivalent. Therefore, -oat convert to 1. This 1 depicts row 1.

To label some of the other squares shown, one could use the following examples:

B1. bat   **B2. bean**   **B3. bomb**
C2. cone   **C3. cam**

To place for instance, book into square B 1, simply associate book with bat. Of course, the number of rows or columns is optional. As with any other peg system, one can link from these pegs. Such a system is applicable to maps, tables and music. In music, one could use this for such aspects as written music and string instrument fingering.

A two dimensional grid system is not the only application for Two Dimensional Pegs. You could use this system on any such number letter combinations. For example, you can use this principle to memorize the apartment number of each tenant living in an apartment building. One way of applying this is to apply letter/number images to the tenants, using the Loci System. A doorman may find this useful.

CHAPTER 21

PLAYING CARDS

Whether one plays cards or not, or intends to in the future, this chapter provides an excellent fun way to develop your memory.

THE CARD ITEM

To apply memory techniques to playing cards, one must first establish in one's mind, a different item for each card of the deck. That is, each card is permanently assigned a unique item. To identify a playing card, only two details are necessary. This is the card's number and its suit. In the system taught here,7 the name of each item depicts these two details of its corresponding card. Of each item's name, the first letter is that of the card's suit, and the other letters in this name depict the card's number by the Phonetic Code. Notice that this is the same principle as that of *Two Dimensional Pegs* of chapter 20. The following is my list of card items.

A♦ date	A♣ cat	A♥ hat	A♠ suit
2♦ dune	2♣ can	2♥ honey	2♠ sun
3♦ dime	3♣ comb	3♥ ham	3♠ sam
4♦ deer	4♣ car	4♥ hair	4♠ sewer
5♦ doll	5♣ coal	5♥ heel	5♠ sail
6♦ dish	6♣ cash	6♥ hash	6♠ sash
7♦ dock	7♣ cake	7♥ hog	7♠ sock
8♦ dove	8♣ coffee	8♥ hoof	8♠ safe
9♦ dope	9♣ cape	9♥ hoop	9♠ soap
10♦ dice	10♣ case	10♥ hose	10♠ suds
J♦ diamond	J♣ club	J♥ heart	J♠ spade
Q♦ drum	Q♣ cream	Q♥ queen	Q♠ stem
K♦ drink	K♣ king	K♥ hinge	K♠ song

For examples, A♦. depicts the ace of diamonds. 2♥ depicts the 2 of hearts (deuce of hearts), J♠ is the Jack of spades and K♣ depicts the King of clubs. For instance, take the word *sail*. The first letter is *s*, which depicts spades. The other letters in the name, *ail*, convert to. 5. Therefore, the word *sail* depicts the 5 of spades.

I realize that you may have noticed some inconsistencies of the rules with the face cards. As you will see, this is of no consequence. There is a small advantage, which is the reason for these inconsistencies. Of course, you can change them to conform. In this case, the numbers for jack, queen and king is 11,12 and 13 respectively.

As for the two jokers in the deck. my card item for the red joker is Batman's enemy *the Joker* (as played by the actor, Cesar Romero). My card item for the black joker is a large plump African American comedian I know.

IN A CARD GAME

To keep track of the distribution of cards in a card game, simply associate the card items to the participants using the Loci System.

For example, let's suppose that during a card game, you witness one of the participant's receiving (or discarding, depending on the game) the two of clubs. You could apply this by imagining, for instance, that a *can* is now sticking out of his or her mouth. Let's suppose that he or she later receives, the queen of clubs. For this, you might then imagine that the can now drips lots of *cream* onto the table. Let's say that you later witness his or her receiving the 3 of clubs. You could then imagine, for instance, that a *comb* is now dancing on his or her shoulder as well.

As you witness the participant's loosing one of these cards, you imagine the card item of that card leaving the scene. For example, you could imagine that that image suddenly blasts off into space or runs away. Of course, you would apply the same techniques to the other participants at the same time. Because this technique involves people, it is important to apply the lessons of Chapter 4.

DETECTING MISSING CARDS

This is a very impressive stunt. This is also useful in some card games. For example, you could use this technique in determining whether certain cards have been discarded. I will explain it as a stunt. In this stunt, you detect missing cards after but one look through the deck. It works as follows:

While looking at each card in the deck, imagine that its card item becomes damaged (mutilated) in some way. For instance, imagine that each becomes burned. When your look through the deck is complete, recall each card item in some order. I do this in ascending order beginning with the diamonds, then the clubs, then the hearts then the spades. A card item that you had not imagined burned would, of course, not be burned upon your recalling it. As you encounter this, you can call out the name of the card or list it.

For accuracy, it is important to learn well the order in which you recall the 52 card items (54 if the jokers are included). You should establish this order well in your mind. It is good to learn to recall the order of these names rapidly. It is even better to learn to rapidly recall in order, the images of these names. Practicing the rapid recall of a set of images in this way is an excellent way to develop the mind.

One of my techniques is to imagine a mutilation taking place, as opposed to imagining an item that is already mutilated. Thus, I see the item change from a normal to mutilated state. This conforms with the lessons of Chapter 4. Another is to imagine doing the mutilating. For example, one could imagine stomping on, biting into or chewing card items. Obviously, this invites the use of other senses such as taste.

One problem may occur when performing this stunt. A person can mistake a certain card item's mutilation during a previous attempt of the stunt, as one during the present attempt. This is so, even if the card in question is one of the missing. To avoid this, you can alternate with at least five different types of mutilation. In other words, you can use a different form of mutilation each time you perform the stunt.

For example, upon your first performance, you imagine that each is burned. Upon the next performance, imagine that each is twisted, and so forth. Other examples of forms of mutilation are: cut up, crushed, stretched, and sprayed with acid. It's even better to try to think continuously of new forms of mutilation. I even use different variations of each type. For example, one variation of cut up may be sliced. Another may be diced. One variation of burned may be torched and another may be grilled. There you go. You have more than enough ideas of mutilation now. Why not use them all? Of course, this method of alternation would also be useful in a card game of numerous sessions.

The following is a version of this stunt that I've created. It does not require the use of a deck of cards. To perform it, the spectators take turns calling out the name of a card of a typical card deck as they attempt to eventually call out all card names of the deck. If one of the spectators calls out a card name that has already been called out during the stunt, you immediately state this fact to the spectators.

What will happen during this stunt is that soon a situation will come whereas almost all the cards the spectators call out are such repeats. At this point, the spectators have the option of either quitting, or continuing. If they succeed in calling out every card name, you immediately announce to them that they have finished. If they quit, you then tell them the card names not called out yet.

The application of memory techniques to this version of the stunt is the same as that of the previous version. Also, for their reference, the spectators should form and maintain a written record of the card names called out.

MEMORIZING THE ORDER OF A SHUFFLED DECK

To memorize the order of a shuffled deck of cards, simply apply the appropriate card items, and in the shuffled order, to a number peg system. As you look through a shuffled deck, you place the card item of each card you see into a peg. The image depicting the first card you see is placed into peg 1, that of the second card is put into peg 2, and so forth. When you have finished placing all 52 card items (54 if the jokers are included), you could quickly determine the place number of any card. For example, if asked what place in the deck is, for instance, the 7 of clubs, you could answer correctly immediately. For this, simply think of the card item (cake), and this would bring to mind the peg in which that image is placed, thus bringing to mind the peg number, which is the answer. Another ability is that given any number from 1 to 52 you could immediately determine the card in that place. Therefore, you could instantly determine which card is, for instance, the 28th card in the deck. For this, you simply think of peg 28, which would of course bring to mind the card item in that peg.

My way of performing this stunt is to have another person recite to me in order, each card of the entire deck. As the person does this, he or she numerically lists each card on a sheet of paper. Then, when anyone present challenges me, he or she uses the list to check my answers. This is much quicker and more convenient than to look through the deck for each answer.

Another way to detect missing cards is to use pegs. All you have to do is place card items into pegs, then review each pegged card item. Do this in the same order as taught in the second and third paragraph of *Detecting missing cards,* which is on page 70. Any card item not placed into any of the pegs, one could detect easily. Thus, you can combine both the missing card and shuffled order stunt. Nevertheless, I've found it easier to do these stunts separately.

The following version of this stunt is another of my creations, and it also does not require a deck of cards. To perform it, you have the spectators take turns calling out the name of a card of a typical card deck, as they attempt to eventually call out all of the card names of that deck. As they call them out, you memorize the listing using the same techniques use in the previous version of the stunt. As they call them out, one spectator should numerically list the cards on a piece of paper pre-numbered according to a pre-determined list length. Then of course, the spectators test your memory of the list, using the written list as a reference.

However, as the spectators call out card names, most likely some card names would be repeated. To handle this, you have two options:

For one, you could simply ignore the fact that it's a repeat and include it in the listing. If you go by this policy, the listing and calling out ends when the spectators have called out a number of card names equal to the pre-determined list length. For this, I recommend the length of the list to be 50 or 100. The length could be the choice of the spectators.

For the other option, upon any such repeat, you immediately stop the calling out and listing of card names. You then tell that spectator that that card name has already been called out, then tell them the list number of that card name. Then you have the spectators continue. If this is the policy, the length of the list is of course 52 (54 if the jokers are included).

DEVELOPING SPEED

I must tell you that to perform any of these stunts with even a minimum of adequate speed, the association of a card with its assigned item must become second nature. In other words, it must be that upon seeing a card, its card item automatically comes to mind.

In addition, the pegs you use, you must know just as well. I therefore recommend practicing the method described in *Developing Speed and Skill with your Pegs,* which is on page 24.

To help in memorizing your card items and their assignments (that is of course, until you're more accustomed to them), I suggest that you use an aid. A method for this that I myself like best is as follows: I set up a card peg system .of which each peg label depicts the card number. Thus there are thirteen pegs and the labels range from *Ace* to *King*. In each peg, I've placed the four card items of that number. For examples, for the Aces, I imagined a fighter plane flying (fighter ace) that shoots delicious *dates* (A♦) being flown by a *cat* (A♣) that is wearing a *suit* (A♠) and a large *hat* (A♥)., For the deuces, I imagined a scene of an open very shiny *can* (2♣) of *honey* (2♥) riding a bicycle (2 wheels) around on some sand *dunes* (2♦), while being chased by a small *sun* (2♠) that is trying to cook the honey.

Each day, look through a shuffled deck of cards while trying to recall each card item. Upon any difficulty recalling a card item with the use of the code itself, review the peg of the card's number. As speed increases, raise the speed standards. When satisfied with your speed, begin a daily schedule of practicing the Missing Card Stunt. Then practice the Card Order Stunt weekly.

When I look at a card, I look only at the top left corner. I do this in case someone challenges me to do stunts with one of those picture decks. Also, I look at the suit before the number.

Many times, I've incorrectly determined a card item of a card because I didn't pay close enough attention to its suit. However, the card numbers have always been correct. From this, I've learned that it's more important to pay close attention to the suit of a card.

As I've just mentioned, of the pegs you use, you must know well.

There are many card stunts a person can perform using these techniques. I'm sure that you can think of some.

OTHER TYPES OF CARD DECKS

Of course, this system can accommodate other card decks. Take for instance, a deck for pinochle. Such a deck has two of each card, and it contains no number cards from 2 through 8.

For a deck such as this, I see, so far, two ways to accommodate. In both, you form a different image word for each twin. In both methods, the first encountered of a pair receives the previous image word; the other receives the new word.

Of the first method, the new image word conforms to the same rules. For two examples, for the ace of spades and the nine of clubs, you can use *seat* and *cap* respectively.

Of the second method, you use the principle of the first method of *Extending a peg list* on page 26. In this case, the twin of, for instance, the ace of clubs is given the image word of *paper cat*.

CHAPTER 23

BINARY AND OCTAL NUMBERS

I've included this chapter to enable you to understand certain systems in Chapters 23 and 26. You could skip this chapter now then refer to it later if and when you find it necessary. Here, I will cover the Binary Number System, then the Octal Number System. Then I will show you how to convert from one to the other. (10010)

Until now, the Binary and Octal Number Systems have been used solely for computer and digital applications. The second paragraph of *For the computer tech* on page 114 is a brief explanation of such applications. Also, in that sub-chapter are ways to apply memory techniques to binary and octal numbers. Well proudly I must say, I've invented uses for both of these number systems for Memory Techniques. To use them effectively for this, one must understand well the concepts of these two number systems.

Certainly, the number counting system most common to all people throughout the world, would consist of ten different characters. For you and me, they are the characters 0 to 9. However, a system comprised of a different number of characters is just as possible. Such a system could consist of, for example, seven different characters (0 to 6).

At first this may seem strange, but now consider this: Think for a minute about the way you first learned to count. For this, you probably used your fingers. This is probably the same for almost every other person who ever lived, including those who had invented our customary number system. Naturally, this number system would consist of ten characters, because a normal human has ten fingers. Now imagine how we probably would count if every human past and present had, for example, twelve fingers instead. If this were so, our number system would most likely consist of twelve characters instead of ten. Now imagine if octopuses used a number system as we do. How many characters would their number system contain? Well, this chapter is basically about other such number systems.

The octal number system is exactly the same as our customary number system, with one exception. It uses eight characters (0 to 7) instead of ten (0 to 9). For better comprehension, notice the right-most vertical set of numbers of *Figure 1*. Notice how they seem to skip over or ignore any numbers consisting of characters 8 and 9. By the way, the octal number system is the system an octopus would probably use.

BASE CONVERSIONS		
10	2	8
0	0	0
1	1	1
2	10	2
3	11	3
4	100	4
5	101	5
6	110	6
7	111	7
8	1000	10
9	1001	11
10	1010	12
11	1011	13
12	1100	14
13	1101	15
14	1110	16
15	1111	17
16	10000	20
17	10001	21
18	10010	22
19	10011	23
20	10100	24

Figure 1

The Binary Number System is exactly the same as both, our customary number system and the octal number system, with one exception. Instead of using ten (or eight) characters, the Binary System uses but two characters (0 to 1). In fact, the preceding paragraph could have just as well pertained to the Binary Number System instead of the Octal Number System by simply changing a few words and numbers to it.

You probably wonder how the Binary System can depict the number two, three, or higher with but two characters. Well, think about the Morse code for a moment. Like the Morse Code, which uses only two characters, (dot and dash), the Binary System uses only two characters as well (which are, zero and one). A typical binary number is 10011. This binary number, for example, is equivalent to the number nineteen.

Because it is comprised of two different characters, the Binary Number System is a base 2 number system. Therefore, our most common number system, known as the Decimal System, is a base 10 system. Likewise, the Octal Number System is a base 8 number system.

I want you now to think for a moment about ordinary counting (0, 1, 2, 3, 4, 5,...) Now imagine counting in this way up to a large number such as one hundred thousand. As you know, the numbers increase in width at certain points. To be more specific, the numbers increase in width by one digit at the count of ten. Then the next width increase is at one hundred. Then the next is at one thousand, and so forth. Well, counting in binary is just like counting in the usual way, but skipping all numbers consisting of characters 2 through 9. Thus, the only characters used are 0 and 1. Therefore, such increases in width would of course occur much more sooner and more frequently. This does not matter, unless of course it is undesirable for a number to have a large width.

Figure 1 on page 75 is a chart from 0 to 20, of the, number systems of bases 10, 2, and 8. For now, ignore the rightmost column (the base 8 column). The center list is that of the binary numbers, and the list to its left is that of our usual number system.

For better comprehension of the Binary System (base 2 system). I've created two exercise to do. Of either exercise, I advise that you use the principles taught in the preceding paragraphs.

Of the first exercise, I also want you to keep in mind that the only possible characters you can use in this exercise are 0 and/or 1. Throughout the exercise ignore the left and right lists of figure 1. Therefore, pay attention only to the center list. I now want you to perform the following steps.

1. Using a piece of paper, cardboard or such, cover the list of numbers in figure one so that of only 0 at the top of the list is showing just above the cardboard.

2. Of this number of the center list that is now showing just above the cardboard, carefully answer to yourself this question:

What is the next higher number that consists of characters of only 0 or 1?

3. Slide the cardboard down so that the next number below it is showing just above the cardboard. If you've already reached the very bottom of the list, go directly to step 6.

4. Compare this number that is now just above the cardboard with the answer you've just derived from the question in step 2.

5. while holding down the cardboard in its present position, go directly back to step 2.

6. Provided you have done the steps correctly, you have moved the cardboard down 20 times, thus moving it down the whole list. In doing this, you would have gained a much better understanding of binary numbers.

The other exercise is as follows:

Imagine that all you had at your desk is the two rubber stampers below, a regular sheet of lined loose leaf paper, and a stamp ink pad.

You are to place consecutive numbers on this sheet of paper from top to bottom on both sides. You are to do it using only the items mentioned. Therefore, the number are to be consecutive, but with one exception, which is that any number that cannot be put onto the sheet (such as those consisting of any characters from 2 thru 9), you are to ignore as you proceed. However, you are to place a number on each and every line (or row) beginning on one side, then continuing the series on the other side. You are to take caution not to exclude any number that can apply. To do the exercise, you could use a pencil or pen instead of the two stampers. That is, if you pretend that the pencil or pen is the two stampers, and therefore, you abide by the rule that this pencil or pen, like the stampers, cannot be used to print any characters other than a 0 or a 1.

If you have done the exercise correctly the first twenty numbers would be exactly like the base 2 numbers of figure 1) Never the less, provided you didn't make too many mistakes, doing this exercise would provide a better understanding of binary numbers.

Notice in figure 1, the patterns of the Binary System as compared with those of the base 10 system to its left. You can use this chart for some number conversions. For instance, suppose that you wish to find the base 2 equivalent of the number nine. For this, you could simply find nine in the left list then look to its right. There, you would find its base 2 equivalent. If you look further right, into the other list, you would find its base 8 equivalent. For better comprehension, I want you now to use this chart to find the base 2 equivalent of the base ten number eighteen. **Do it now.** The answer is at the end of the first paragraph of this chapter.

Converting from binary to octal is simple, and I will explain it by example. For an example, consider the binary number 11101010110. To convert it to octal, first separate the digits, from right to left, into groups of three as follows:

11 101 010 110

Finally, change each group to its octal equivalent (Refer to figure 1.). In doing this, the result would be 3526(base 8).

From this example, you've probably already figured out how to do the reverse process. You simply change each octal digit to its binary three digit equivalent. By the term three digit equivalent, I mean that each octal digit converts to a three digit number. As you know, to do this, you simply place one or two zeros to the left of the binary digit or digits, when it is necessary. Such is the case with the third octal digit from the left. Of course you need not apply this to the left most octal digit. For better comprehension, try these methods with some of the numbers in figure 1. At this point, I suggest that you again review what we've covered.

The rest of this chapter covers a quick method of these conversions, and without the use of such a chart as that in figure 1. However, to learn the method, you must first understand well some numerical principles:

To begin, I wish to make sure that you understand the meaning of powers. I can show this best by example. Let's suppose that N is any number of your choice. Then N to the first power is simply N. N to the second power is N × N. N to the third power is N × N × N, and so on. Notice the pattern. Therefore, 5 to the 4th power, for example, equals 5 × 5 × 5 × 5, which of course equals 25 × 5 × 5, which of course equals 25 × 25, which of course equals 125 × 5, which of course equals 625. For another example, 10 to the 3rd power is 10 × 10 × 10 which equals 1000.

There is one rule that I will not try to explain. Never the less, the rule is: any number (N) to the zero power always equals 1. Therefore, seventeen (for an example) to the zero power, equals one. Just keep this rule in mind throughout the lessons. The only exception to this rule is that if the number (N) is zero, this rule does not apply. Such a result is impossible. Therefore, zero to the zero power could not exist.

As I've said, all of these number systems are alike with but one exception. Therefore, the principles of number place holders correspond. As you most likely know, in our Base Ten System, each digit is multiplied by the power of ten corresponding to the digit's place or column. Going **from right to left**, such powers of ten are 0, 1, 2, 3, and so on. Then the results of these multiplication's are added. In doing this, you would of course derive the original number.

To see this in action, let's take for example, the number 7309. The entire operation is as follows:

7		3		0		9		
x 1000		x100		x10		x1		
7000	+	300	+	0	+	9	=	7309

Notice that the right most digit (9) is multiplied by ten to the zero power. The next digit (0) is multiplied by ten to the first power. The digit next to that (3) is multiplied by ten to the second power, and so on. Notice also how the results (bottom numbers) are added (from left to right).

For better comprehension, I suggest that you try this procedure on some whole numbers of three digits or more.

The same principles apply to a number of another base, again with one exception. Instead of powers of ten, it works in powers of whatever base the number is of. Also, all the numbers in the procedure must be in the form of that base.

Likewise, the same principles apply to a binary number, again with one exception. Instead of powers of ten, it works in powers of two. Also, all the numbers in the procedure, including the powers of two, must be in their base 2 form.

Therefore, the powers of two would be as follows:

10000   1000   100   10   1

Notice that these numbers look exactly like the powers of ten in the procedure above. These numbers could even be mistaken for those in that procedure very easily. However, remember that these are binary numbers. In base ten, they are: 16 8 4 2 1. For better comprehension, refer to the chart of figure 1 to confirm this.

To see the procedure in action, let's apply it to the number 1011(base2). It works as follows:

$$\begin{array}{ccccccccc}
1 & & 0 & & 1 & & 1 & & \\
\underline{\times 1000} & & \underline{\times 100} & & \underline{\times 10} & & \underline{\times 1} & & \\
1000 & + & 0 & + & 10 & + & 1 & = & 1011
\end{array}$$

Again, notice each power of two going from right to left. As you can see, we have again derived the original number.

We will now use the principles in the lesson I've just given. We will use them to convert a number from base two to base ten. For the conversion, all we need do is to make a slight change in the procedure. This change is that the powers of two are in their base 10 form instead. Thus, these powers would be as follows:

16 8 4 2 1

To see the procedure in action, let's apply it to the same binary number, to convert it to its base ten form. Again, the number is 1011(base2).

$$\begin{array}{ccccccccc}
1 & & 0 & & 1 & & 1 & & \\
\underline{\times 8} & & \underline{\times 4} & & \underline{\times 2} & & \underline{\times 1} & & \\
8 & + & 0 & + & 2 & + & 1 & = & 11(base10)
\end{array}$$

Again, notice each power of two. Therefore, 1011(base 2) is equivalent to 11(base 10). I strongly suggest that you practice this conversion method because you will use it. You should become well accustomed to it. For better comprehension, try the procedure on binary numbers with the powers of two written in base 8. In doing this, you would convert the binary number to its octal form.

Practice with numbers of 10100(base 2) (equivalent to 20) or lower and refer to figure 1 to check your answers. At this point, you should again review what you have just learned.

For the techniques in this book, it is essential to know how to do the calculation I've just covered. Nevertheless, the techniques in this book do not require converting any numbers to or from base 10. They require only conversions from base 2 to base 8 or visa versa. Therefore, for our purpose, we need only to concern ourselves with numbers of 7 (111 in base 2) or lower.

To see the advantage of this, first notice in figure 1 the numbers **0**(base 10) to **7**(base 10). Now notice there that each of these is identical to its base 8 equivalent. Now recall the part of the lesson on binary to octal conversion (on page 77) in which I said that the **binary** digits are separated into groups of three, then each is converted. Therefore, converting each group to either base 10 or base 8 would have the same result. In addition, each resulting digit would be within the boundaries of 0 to 7.

Therefore, to convert a large binary number to its octal equivalent, you can do the following: Using part of the method on page 77, you first separate the binary digits from right to left into groups of three. Then on each group, you use the calculation above to find each octal digit. It's that simple.

With a little practice, you could easily do such conversions quickly and mentally. Also with such practice, you would naturally learn how to do the reverse process just as easily. With but a little practice, you would find that the most difficult part of it all is simply the adding of up to three possible numbers. Of course these numbers are 4, 2, and 1, of which it is simple to add any of them together.

To use binary to octal conversions effectively in the memory techniques, I suggest that you practice it to the point whereas you can do it all mentally.

One good way to practice is to do so on long binary numbers that you select at random. To check your answers, use a calculator that can automatically do such calculations. The most up to date scientific calculators should have such features. Some models are inexpensive and they are available in such places as department and electronics stores. Just make sure that the calculator has such features before you purchase it.

Naturally, there's more to such number systems than that which I've covered here. I haven't covered such subjects as their arithmetic, and the conversion from base 10 to one of the others. I've covered only what is necessary to understand the subject matter in this book. Nevertheless, if you wish to learn more about this, I suggest that you consult one or more books that cover computer or digital mathematics.

On second thought, I might as well show you how to convert a base 10 number to one of the other bases. Of course, you don't need to know this to understand the book's subject matter. I've included it just for those who want to know how to do it.

Basically, to convert such a number, you continuously divide the number by the new base until there is nothing left. As you do this, you collect each remainder (including zeros) and keep them in the order in which you find them. This collection of remainders would be the number in the new base. The first remainder you find would be the right most digit, and so on.

To see this in action, let's convert 83 to its base 2 form. I will show the procedure in steps, and it is as follows (Study the last step carefully.):

STEPS
↓
1. $83 \div 2 = 41$ with a remainder of 1 (right most digit)
2. $41 \div 2 = 20$ 1
3. $20 \div 2 = 10$ 0
4. $10 \div 2 = 5$ 0
5. $5 \div 2 = 2$ 1
6. $2 \div 2 = 1$ 0
7. $1 \div 2 = 0$ .... 1 (left most digit)

Therefore, 1010011(base 2) is equivalent to 83(base 10). When practicing the procedure, you could check your answer by converting the result back to its original form, using a previous procedure. Try using this procedure to convert 83 to its base 8 form. In this case you divide by 8 in each step instead of by 2. Also in this case, a remainder could be any number from 0 to 7.

To understand the concepts even more, try the procedure on 83, but divide by 10 in each step. In this case, you should derive the same number in the same form.

The following is an exercise for practice. The answers are on page 163.

Now examine the base 8 numbers (octal numbers) of figure 1 and compare its pattern with that of the binary system. At this point, you should review and study all we've just covered because to understand the following lessons, it is important that you understand well, the concepts I've just taught.

Convert each number to its other form of either binary or octal. In this exercise, (2) depicts that the number is of base 2, whereas (8) depicts that it is of base 8.

1. 7541(8)
2. 10110000(2)
3. 7010(8)
4. 1001101101(2)
5. 1234(8)
6. 1001000001(2)
7. 747(8)
8. 4321(8)
9. 1011(8)
10. 101001001(2)
11. 11010111110(2)
12. 1110001010(2)
13. 1011111(2)
14. 1100111(2)
15. 3173(8)

Chapter 23

CODES

This chapter provides another excellent way to practice the systems. As I have stated, my application of a code is similar to my application of a language. Therefore, for each individual code of the set,

I would associate the name of the set of codes, the code, and its meaning together. As you will see in later chapters, the memory techniques used here are adaptable to other subjects and applications.

As in all codes, you should be careful of your choice of backgrounds of your imaginary scenes. Never choose a background that pertains to the image common in all the scenes. In this case, the image is that of the name of the set of codes. Such images, that you will find in this chapter, are: walkie talkie, signaling flag and seeing eye dog. For example, a scene that you are likely to find a signaling flag, such as on an aircraft carrier, would be a bad choice. Instead, choose a background that pertains to one of the other two images. Thus, all of your scenes would be different, and this would prevent confusion.

NUMBER CODE SYSTEMS

One example of a code is the CB and police radio code. Anyone who is familiar with CB radio or the popular quotation "10-4," which means acknowledgment, knows of this code.

First, each element begins with 10. Therefore, only the succeeding number needs attention.

To recall that 10-16 indicates a domestic dispute, you could imagine that in a house made of porcelain (dish for 16), a walkie talkie (radio code) is trying to settle a noisy dispute between a couple. To recall that 10-14 indicates a prowler's presence, one could imagine that a woman walkie talkie is afraid. She is afraid because a tire (14) is prowling around her home. The recall of this is the same as that for a language. As you probably see, this is but another number peg system.

In case you want to know the rest of the code, the list under this paragraph is the information I have. You should try the system out, if for no other reason, to see how well the technique works. Test yourself by trying to recall the code numbers to definitions, and visa versa, in random order. This is also the applies to the entire chapter.

10-01 poor signal
10-02 good signal
10-03 stop transmission
10-04 acknowledgment
10-05 relay
10-06 busy if not urgent
10-07 leaving site
10-08 returning to site
10-09 repeat message
10-10 fight
10-11 fire
10-12 standby
10-13 need assistance
10-14 prowler
10-15 riot or crowd
10-16 domestic dispute
10-17 complaint
10-18 police at scene
10-19 return to ...
10-20 location
10-21 phone call
10-22 disregard
10-23 arriving at scene
10-24 assignment complete
10-25 escort
10-32 person with gun
10-36 correct time
10-37 status report
10-38 injured person
10-39 officer down
10-41 need supervision
10-50 need police
10-51 need paramedics
10-99 bomb threat
10-100 personal

MORSE CODE SYSTEMS

The following are four systems I've created for memorizing the International Morse Code. You can of course choose any one of them. Also, you do not necessarily need to use the same system for each and every letter. For most of these systems, you must know the Phonetic Code System well. If you look, you would see that except for one of them, each of these systems is basically a peg system of which the peg labels are the letters of the alphabet.

These next two paragraphs are an explanation of the Morse Code System. Using the Morse Code, a message is sent one letter at a time. Each letter or punctuation mark, in Morse code is a unique combination of dots and dashes. A dot is an abrupt audible tone. That is, a tone that lasts for a minute amount of time. A dash is- exactly the same except that it lasts for twice to three times the time of a dot. Of course, there's a sufficient time interval between each letter, and there's a slightly longer time interval between each word. The Morse code equivalent of, for example, A is • — (dot dash). The equivalent of, for example R is • — • (dot dash dot).

Instead of audible tones, one could transmit a Morse code message in the form of light flashes, using, for example, a flashlight. Another way is to use a flag. For this, a dot is a figure eight flag waving to the sender's right, whereas a dash is one to the left. Between each letter or symbol, the sender momentarily holds the flag straight up. Such is the general idea of the Morse Code System.

This first system, took the most work to develop. In this chapter and Chapter 26, I show adaptations of it for use in other fields. I will now repeat my advice that to comprehend a system more easily, it sometimes helps to draw your own diagrams as you proceed. In my explanation of this system, the term character refers to a dot or a dash.

Each character is assigned a digit. The digits then convert to their phonetic code equivalent. Then one creates an imaginary scene that associates this result with two other elements, which are: the code's name (Morse Code) and the letter it depicts. For the letter, I use an image from my alphabet list on page 37. Such is the general idea of the system.

The digit assignment and word coding process is as follows: First, the characters are to be separated into groups of two. For the first group from left to right, any dot in it is changed to a 1, and any dash in it is changed to a 2. Then the resulting digits are converted to one word. For the next group, any dot is changed to a 3, and any dash is changed to a 4. Then this result is also converted to one word. The two words are then put together. For speed in finding the proper words, I use only image words listed in my Phonetic Code Peg List (on page 51).

Now for an example of this process. Take the letter B. In Morse code, the letter B is — • • •. To begin, separating the characters into twos, I obtain (— •) (• •). Accordingly, the first or leftmost group (— •) is changed to 21. 21 then converts to its word in my peg list (wand). Then the next group (• •) is changed to 33, which then convert to its word (mummy). Placing the two words together, I derive *wand mummy.*

The following is my morse code list for the alphabet. For better comprehension, I suggest that you examine them all for consistency with the lesson.

A.	• —	(tin)	N.	— •	(wand)
B.	— • • •	(wand mummy)	O.	— — —	(nun hair)
C.	— • — •	(wand rum)	P.	• — — •	(tin rum)
D.	— • •	(wand ham)	Q.	— — • —	(nun hammer)
E.	•	(tie)	R.	• — •	(tin ham)
F.	• • — •	(tooth rum)	S.	• • •	(tooth ham)
G.	— — •	(nun ham)	T.	—	(honey)
H.	• • • •	(tooth mummy)	U.	• • —	(tooth hair)
I.	• •	(tooth)	V.	• • • —	(tooth.. hammer)
J.	• — — —	(tin rower)	W.	• — —	(tin hair)
K.	— • —	(wand hair)	X.	— • • —	(wand hammer)
L.	• — • •	(tin mummy)	Y.	— • — —	(wand rower)
M.	— —	(nun)	Z.	— — • •	(nun mummy)

The next step is to form an imaginary scene for each alphabet letter, which in this case makes 26 scenes. As I had implied, such a scene associates three elements. These are: the word coding derived in the process I've just explained, *Morse Code,* and the alphabet letter.

Let's suppose that one's image for *Morse Code* is that of a signaling flag. To apply this system to, for instance, the letter Q, you are to form a mental scene that combines *signal flag, radio dial* (from page 37) and an image of your idea of *nun hammer.*

For example, a person could imagine a *nun* who is nailing big shinny *radio knobs* onto her *signaling flag.* She wants the flag to rattle and reflect light when she signals. She also thinks that because the knobs are from radios, they will reflect radio waves. To add more absurdity to the scene, one could imagine that the hammer she is using is a *nun hammer.* It is partially encased in a tiny nun's habit and its ivory handle has carvings of appropriate religious designs and symbols. In it, there is a compartment for holy water, from which the water can leak out onto the item she repairs. Thus, it automatically blesses the item as well.

For the letter H, a person could imagine that a thick yellow *ladder* is trying to signal for help, using a large *signal flag*. A *tooth mummy* is chasing the ladder, to bite it with its huge chattering fang like teeth. The mummy smells musty, as they usually do.

In the next paragraph, is an example of the use of this system to recall the character combination of a particular letter. Then in the paragraph following it, is an example of the use of the system to recall the letter of a particular character combination.

To recall, for instance, the Morse Code equivalent of Q, the person is to think of what scene it is in which *radio dial* is combined with *signal flag* (Morse Code). The scene of the nun using the hammer would come. Because of the system, it could only be nun hammer. *Nun hammer* converts back to its phonetic code equivalent, 22 34. Applying the digit assignment process in reverse, 22 34 converts back to − − • −

To recall the letter equivalent of the character combination: • • • •, begin by applying the digit assignment process to these characters, thus converting them to 11 33. Then convert the result to the phonetic code equivalent. Because only listed peg words apply here, one would quickly derive *tooth mummy*. Then think of what scene it is in which *tooth mummy* is combined with *signal flag*. The scene with the ladder would come to mind. Therefore, the letter H would come to mind.

Given any combination of dots and dashes, you can quickly find the proper words, and their correct order. Finding the correct order is simple. For this, when you have converted the words of a morse code letter to digits, you simply put the digit pairs (groups or two) in order from left to right with the lower number pair first. As you probably see, only twelve of the phonetic code peg words are used here, which simplifies the search for the proper words. The entire recall process may seem slow and laborious. However, one who understands the system can easily do the process quickly and mentally.

I want you now to notice something about this system. In light of the first four paragraphs about it (beginning on page 84), all **dots** automatically convert to digits that are **odd** numbers. In turn, all **dashes** convert to **even** number digits. This aspect is very useful. Take for example the series 2134. With this aspect in mind, it is probably obvious to you that 2134 converts back to − • • −. 133 back to • • •, and 1134 back to • • • −. This can help you to quickly convert from the digits to characters or visa versa. It is also useful in checking whether such conversions are correct.

I've included the following in case you want the rest of the code:

```
1  • − − − −      6  − • • • •      ,  − − • • − −      !  • − • • − −
2  • • − − −      7  − − • • •      .  • − • − • −      '  • − − − − •
3  • • • − −      8  − − − • •      ?  • • − − • •      -  − • • • • −
4  • • • • −      9  − − − − •      ;  − • − • − •      /  − • • − • −
5  • • • • •      0  − − − − −      :  − − − • • •      (  − • − − • −
```

Applying my system to any of these causes the existence of a third group pair consisting of the 5th and 6th characters. Of this group, you change any dot to a 5, and any dash to a 6. Of course, the phonetic code word derived from this group would always be the last word of the three. For examples, the image words for a question mark (?) would be *tooth rower lily*. In turn, those for a period would be *tin hammer leash*. For another example, a colon would be *nun rum lily*. You may find it unnecessary to apply the system to the characters depicting the number digits because of their pattern.

This second system for the Morse Code I've thought of after seeing a logo on television. I can explain it best by example. For an example, imagine the Morse Code characters of a Q with its ends rolled up. You might imagine the left figure at the bottom of this paragraph. Does it not resemble a Q? Imagine the characters of an 0 with its ends rolled up in the same way. Two other examples are, if we slant the Morse Code characters of a W and an A, the results may look like the figures to the right of the Q figure.

Now for the third system, which I favor the most. Your efficiency at this system depends on your skill in using the Binary and Octal Number Systems. To learn about such number systems refer to Binary and Octal Numbers on page 75.

For each morse code character combination, take the following steps:

- Count from left to right, the number of dashes there are before the first dot. Then keep this number in mind.

- Change each dot to a 1, and each dash to a 0 (Thus, changing it to a binary number). Then convert this to its octal equivalent.

- Place this octal number to the right of the number derived in the first step.

- Convert the result to its phonetic code equivalent in as few words as possible.

- Associate the result with both the letter and the Morse Code System, using of course an imaginary scene.

For examples, B (— • • •) converts to 17, which could then convert to *tack*. C (— • — •) converts to 15, which can become *tail*. A colon (— — — • • •) converts to 37, which can become *mug*, and U (• • —) converts to 06, which can become *switch*.

After you've done all these conversions, you have the option of omitting the first zero in any of the two digit codes that begin with a zero. For examples, instead of 06 for U, it could be 6. For P, one could use 9 instead of 09. Whether or not you use this option for any of them, you can avoid a conflict by always applying the following rule of this system:

When you encounter an octal code of two or more digits, the first digit is the number of dashes preceding the rest of the morse code letter. For example, the octal code of 23 converts to — — 3, to — — 11, to — — • •. At this point in the book, I am sure that you know how to work out the rest of the details.

This fourth system is a somewhat simple idea. It works as follows: Of this system, the image depicting the Morse Code signal (dot and dash combination) is but a portion of a familiar musical tune. Of this system the time duration of the musical notes are the same as that of the signal.

It could be the very first notes of a particular song. It could be the part of a song that stands out the most, whatever.

Take for instance, the letter V (• • • —). First, I hope that you are familiar with the musical composition, Beethoven's fifth symphony. You probably are, because it is a very popular musical piece in America. Nevertheless, I will continue the lesson as if you were familiar with it.

Notice that the time durations of the very first four notes of this symphony is exactly the same as that of the signal for V. In fact, most of this symphony consists of repetitions of notes of this combination of time durations.

Therefore, in the imaginary scene, This music itself could represent the signal. To associate the signal, V and Morse Code, I could imagine the following:

Beethoven is conducting an orchestra playing this symphony. He is wearing a down coat instead of a tuxedo (I don't want any confusion with this scene and that for W. Instead of a baton, he is using a huge telegraph key press (A device with a key to tap on to send Morse Code) that is wired to each musician. Their hair styles are the shape of huge v shaped antennas, which transmit the music to radios everywhere. What makes this music and scene more effective is that one can also use violin in the association.

BRAILLE

I've included this application in an attempt to show you that the applications of Memory Techniques are truly unlimited. At this point, you probably can derive your own way of applying such techniques to this application. Nevertheless, I will now touch on a few ways.

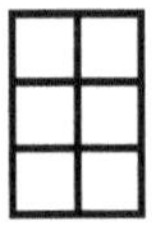

Basically, Braille is a system of writing for blind people. It consists of raised bumps on stiff paper of which a blind person reads by feeling with his or her fingertips. Each letter in Braille is a combination of such bumps in a small two by three grid arrangement such as the figure on the right side of this paragraph. This makes six grid positions. However, the grid is much smaller. In most cases, the grid is about 1/8 inches by 1/4 inches. The following are some braille alphabet characters:

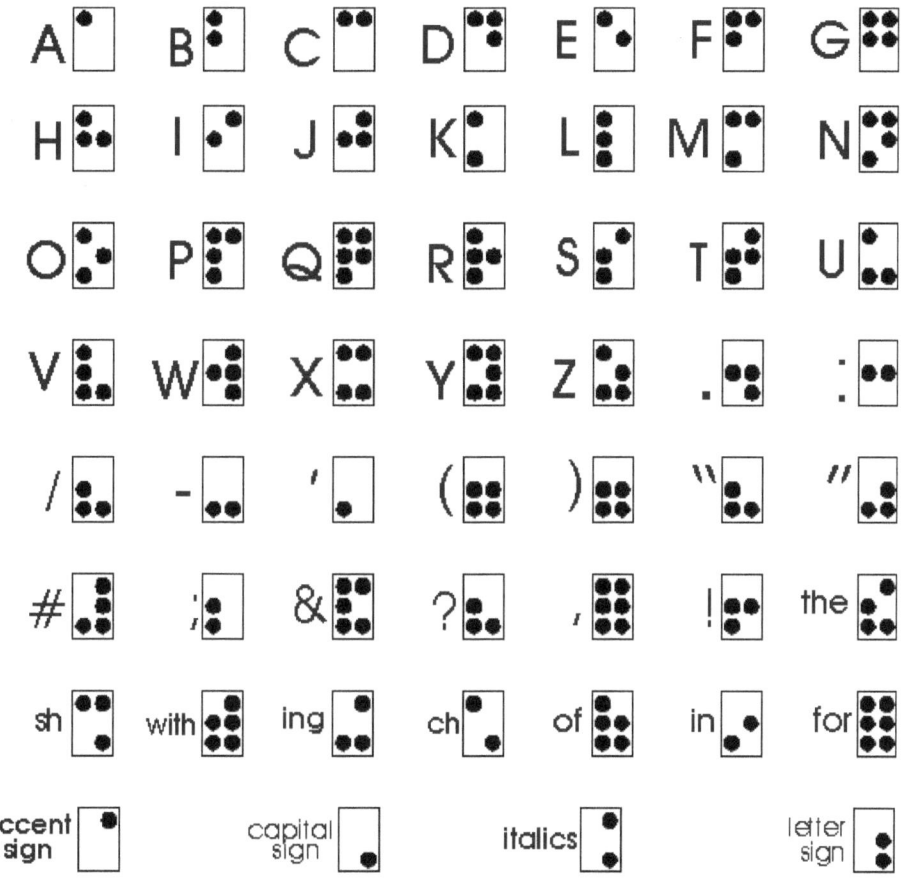

The words **guitar strings** in Braille would be exactly like this:

To depict a series of number digits (1 to 9), letters A to I are preceded by the # character. Therefore, in Braille, #A is 1, #B is 2, #C is 3, etc. Other examples are: #CE is 35, #DA is 41, #EBB is 522, etc. For zero, the J is used. For example, #EJ is 50 and #DJI is 409. The last digit in the series is followed by a space.

For a series of characters such as 2BC125E4AX9, each group of numbers is preceded by the # character, and each• group of letters is preceded by the letter sign. For the lessons here, let's suppose that the letter sign in standard writing is £ (find tha letter sign among the Braille alphabet characters). Thus, the series 2AB125E49 would be written for Braille as: #B£AB#ABE~E#DI. Now carefully compare this series with the number/letter series it came from.

There is much more to Braille than that which I've covered in this book. There are many more characters and combinations. However, to cover it all, it is necessary to go beyond the scope of this book.

So far, I see three ways of applying a memory technique. For one way, you could simply assign a phonetic code number to each of the six grid positions.

A more efficient system is to adapt one of the Morse Code Memory Systems to it. The first of those systems applies well. To apply this system, I would consider a grid position with a bump in it a dot, and an empty grid position a dash.

The two top grid positions depict the first and second characters from left to right. The two center positions in turn depict the third and forth characters and the two bottom positions depict the fifth and sixth characters. Again, for better comprehension, draw your own diagrams of this.

For examples, using the first Morse Code System, R converts to *tin mummy leash,* W converts to *wand mummy jail,* X becomes *tooth rower lily,* and G becomes *tooth mummy judge.*

To form a scene for, for instance, the letter G, you could imagine that a *mummy judge* is sitting at a judge's bench. At the bench, he has a gigantic *microscope* (G) and is trying to place a *seeing eye dog* (Braille) onto it for observation. Both the mummy and the dog have huge *fang like teeth* and are trying to bite each other in the process.

Here are two options you can apply to any of the letters when using this system. One could omit a dash if it is in the last position (sixth position). For example, for R, you could use *tin mummy wool* instead. The other option is that you could omit any dashes if they are of a pair (top pair, middle or bottom pair). For example, X could convert to *tooth lily* instead.

I like this next system the most. It seems to be the most efficient. To use it effectively, you must be very good at working with binary and octal numbers (Refer to *Binary and Octal Numbers* on page 75.). Again, for a better comprehension, draw your own diagrams as you study this subject matter.

In this system, for each letter, you simply convert the bumps and spaces to ones and zeros respectively. Then you convert the result to its octal equivalent. This octal number, you then convert to its phonetic code peg word. For these lessons, I use my own phonetic code peg words, which are on page 51.

However, the grid is arranged in two columns instead of three rows. The left column from bottom to top is for the 1st, 2nd, and 3rd binary digits respectively. In turn, the right column is for the 4th, 5th, and 6th binary digits from bottom to top. If you were to re-arrange the six boxes of the grid horizontally, the bottom left box would contain the 1st digit and the top right box would contain the 6th digit.

The following are examples of such conversions:

A: rice (40 in octal)   D: roach   FOR: cake
W: neck (27 in octal)   V: coyote   S: hammer

Of course the next step is to form imaginary scenes of which each combines the letter, the conversion and the symbol of Braille. I wont you now to figure out the rest of the details on your own. At this point, you have all the necessary knowledge to do so.

CHAPTER 24

CHILDREN AND GAMES

One can teach children all the memory techniques, although some children may be too young for certain lessons, such as the Phonetic System. In this chapter, I cover methods I use to teach such memory techniques to children. I've found that the lessons here apply best to people over the age of eight, which is about the age whereas most become literate. Nevertheless, the minimum requirement for learning the lessons is the ability to do simple addition and subtraction. This chapter also contains fun games to which children can learn to apply such techniques. Adults would find these games fun also. Some of the games in this chapter may be too advanced for young children.

I recommend that you teach children Memory Techniques in the manner depicted in the paragraphs that follow. However, as you proceed, you must also instruct them to use their imaginations to associate the pertinent items in any way they wish. In addition, you should instruct them to include aspects listed in Chapter 4. Statements that are effective for this are: "It's in a scene all to itself." "You can see it move around. "It is colorful.". "you can hear the noise it's making." and so forth. In the beginning, you should give suggestions of imaginary scenes. However, any additional suggestions probably won't be necessary and may cause a decrease in the children's interest. This also applies to the instructions on the use of imagination. During the instructions, it helps to have a few children explain their imaginary scenes. However, one should also insist that each waits for his or her turn. One should also test them to monitor their progress.

One should first teach children the Link System. This requires little if any sort of illustrating. The blackboard illustrating I've found most effective is to draw circles side by side and placing two large bold dots in each. This I would do as I instruct the children to imagine the scenes. Of course, the circles depict the scenes and the dots depict the items in the scenes. Of course, I would then proceed, which includes questioning, testing, and exercises.

For the next technique to teach them, I recommend both the Loci and the Roman Room System as taught on page 34. For this, I've found it most effective to tag stationary items around the room with numbers. The numbers should be placed in accordance with the lessons on the Roman Room System, and I would have at least fifteen items so numbered. These numbered items are of course the pegs. Also, make sure that the numbers are easily visible to all the children as they sit in their seats. Then you could proceed by having the children by your instructions apply to these pegs, a list you make up of random items. I usually use a list of cartoon characters and animals. I first apply the list choosing the tagged places in a random order. Of course, I would then proceed, which includes questioning, testing, and more exercises. I would choose such children at random to answer questions about the list. When you are sure that they are familiar enough with every peg location, remove the tags then test their recall again.

I recommend the Story Method as the next system the children learn. For this, I usually write down a list of items as I and the children make it up. Then I instruct the children in the application of the Story Method to memorizing this list. Then of course I erase the list then test the children's recall.

When they have learned how to apply the Story Method to memorizing lists, I recommend teaching them how to apply it to memorizing telephone numbers. Of course, you could use only items that resemble numbers if the children do not know the concepts of rhyming. Nevertheless, I've found the use of rhyming items more effective. However, it's quite possible for you to teach them the concepts of rhyming. For teaching this method, I recommend using in your lessons statements such as: *Shoe* tree *door gun hive sticks heaven,* show them the similarity between the sounds of these words to the sound of the numbers.

If and when you are confident that the children have learned the previous lessons well, I recommend that you then proceed to teach them the other peg systems. One of my ideas to teach children the basic number peg system is to have them create their own number peg lists. After all, a list that one creates one's self, one would memorize more easily. The following is such a procedure:

Have each child sit at a table with a pencil and lined paper. Have each of them number down the left side of his or her paper from 0 to 9. Then have each write by each number the name of an item that he or she thinks that number looks like. Thus, each child would form his or her own peg list of items that resemble numbers. If you are certain that the children understand what rhyming is, you could apply items that rhyme in the same way. In this case, make sure that the children understand that the rhyming words are to be objects and not terms, and, of course, make sure that they know the difference. You could have them create both types.

So that they understand what they are to write down, it is best to first have them look at a largely written number on display such as on a blackboard. Tell them the number it is, then tell them to think of an object that it also looks like to them. Have them one at a time tell their answers and give your own suggestions. Do this for all the numbers.

Another aid in teaching children the basic number peg system is to use flash cards of number peg labels. Flash cards are easy to make by gluing picture clip-outs' to pieces of cardboard. Such pictures you can take from a combination of sources such as books, magazines, advertisements, photocopies or drawings. Such pictures and cards should be large and legible. Cartoon pictures are very good. There are many places where one can obtain photocopy enlargements, and in color also.

It is a good idea to change peg labels of Chapter 6 on page 20 to words you approve of for children. An example is the word *gun.* For this reason, I've already changed *wine* to *sign.* Therefore, perhaps you might consider changing *gun* to something else, such as *nun* or *sun.* Also, one should make sure that none of the labels are confusing to the children. For instance, one may consider changing *Pharaoh* to *hero,* of which this could refer to a super hero.

My application of Memory Techniques to memorizing multiplication tables is just like that for a code or language. Likewise using this system, you form a scene for each multiplication you wish to apply. Therefore, of a scene for memorizing a multiplication of two numbers, you need to include four elements. The four elements are: the two numbers to multiply, the result, and something that indicates the term multiplication.

For the two numbers to multiply, I use one of the peg lists on page 20 within Chapter 6. For the result, I use another type of peg list such as my phonetic code peg list on page 51. For the term multiplication, I include an action of the production of a large quantity of the item depicting the result.

For an example, take the following multiplication:

9 × 8 = 72

In this case, the two numbers to multiply are 9 and 8, and the result is 72. For this, Lets suppose that I chose to use the first peg list on page 20 and my phonetic code peg list on page 51. I would imagine a scene such as the following:

```
A rope lasso (9) is trying to catch an hour glass (8). The hour glass is
constantly spitting out a bunch of wagons (72) of all kinds.
Each time the lasso tries, it catches instead one or more of
the wagons.
```

To use the system to recall the product of 9 and 8, simply think of the scene that consists of a lasso and an hour glass. The scene of the previous paragraph would come to mind. If you know these peg lists (or any two pegs lists you use) well, you would find this system quite efficient. For the multiplication of a two digit number, such as in the case of 12 × 7, I would add the first peg list on page 20, and image for 12. The number 12 looks to me like a woodpecker on a tree trunk. Therefor, this would be the image I would use in the scene as one of the numbers to multiply.

There are other lessons in this book that would help children and students in their school work, as well as other aspects of their lives. One should also teach children how to apply the Story Method to long digit numbers. They can learn the other lessons of the book, such as the application of such techniques to remembering people and memorizing languages. The Morse Code Memory Systems of Chapter 23 are fun for children. Many models of toy walkie talkies have Morse Code features and it's a good idea to teach the children how to use them if you can.

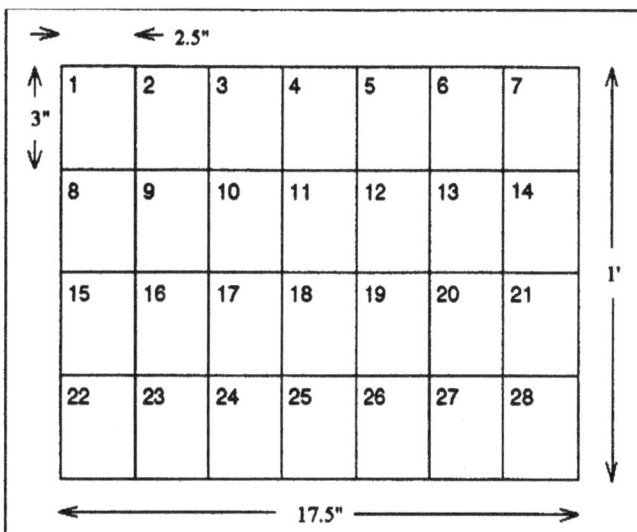

Take a large sheet of paper or cardboard and size and mark it such as that in the diagram above. The sizes in this diagram are but approximate sizes. You can change one or more of those dimensions slightly if you wish to. Now that I think of it, instead of making this sheet, you can use a large planning calendar that has approximately the same size squares. In this case, you simply cross out the squares not used. In addition, the numbers and squares do not necessarily need to be of the same relative positions at those in this diagram.

Figure 2

When the children have learned the peg labels well, they could then be taught how to apply the labels to the Peg System. When they have learned all systems you can start playing with them the games of this chapter. However, one must first be sure that the children know how to apply the appropriate technique to a particular game.

All of the games of this chapter are that of which memorization is a significant factor in winning. Also, with each game, I describe how to apply Memory Techniques to it. Applying Memory Techniques to these games would dramatically increase the changes of winning. However, The techniques may render some of these games too easy for the user. Nevertheless, I will cover them.

Besides, anyone using such techniques would still have fun playing them, especially children. The user could impress the other players who may not know the techniques. The user would even be impressed at both him or herself, and the effectiveness of the techniques. These games are excellent ways the test the techniques, to develop the mind, and to build skill and confidence. This applies especially to children. In addition, playing some of these games and using the techniques them would definitely help you to mentally establish your peg sets. This applies especially to the games near the end of the chapter.

In any of the games that are applicable, instead of using a pen and paper for keeping scores, you can use coins or poker chips, such as, giving a poker chip to a player for scoring a point. In such a case, at the end of the game, the player with the highest stack of such is the winner. In such a case, I recommend a limited number of such chips or coins to hand out, according to the desired length of time of the game.

The Link System can apply to an old game in which each player takes his or her turn repeating a list of items. The player repeating the list then adds another item to the end of it. Therefore, the list continuously increases as the game goes on. A player who makes a mistake is immediately disqualified and the last player left in the game is the winner.

One fun way to play this game is for the players to consider themselves shopping together in a shopping mall. In this case, the list of items is the merchandise. For instance, the first player could say "We went to the mall and bought a pair of Superman boots." The next player could then say "We went to the mall and bought a pair of Superman boots and a lobster." The next player could then say "We went to the mall and bought a pair of Superman boots, a lobster, and a gorilla cage" and the game goes on and on in this way.

This game can be discontinued and continued at any times. Therefore, the game can go on for months or even longer. To eliminate confusion or doubt, you could form and maintain a written record as the game proceeds. As a player is reciting the list, the player who has gone before him or her observes and updates the record and tells all whether the player's recital is correct.

The following is an additional rule you could include.: If a player wishes to remain in the game after he or she has just made an error, the player must correctly recite the entire list backwards. This otherwise difficult task is quite easy when using the Link System.

There are many possible variations of this game. Instead of an unlimited variety of items, the list could consist of other things. It could consist of integers set to a limited range. For example, the range could be from three to seven. Of course it could be from zero to nine as well.

The list could consist of musical tones as played on an instrument such as a piano or xylophone. The instrument could be a toy.

This is the same principle as that of the electronic toy game Simon. This game is a small case with four large buttons of different colors on its top. The game is usually played by one person. Each button when pressed, lights up and sounds a tone different from that of the other buttons.

The game starts with one of the buttons lighting up and sounding its tone. The player must then press that button. The game then repeats its previous action then lights up and tones either the same or another button. The player must then press the buttons in the same sequence in which they have just lit up. The game then repeats its previous action then lights up and tones another or one of the same buttons. The player must then repeat this sequence, which is now three pushes of the buttons. Of course the game continues in this way and the sequence continuously increases.

The moment the player presses a button wrong from the sequence, the game sounds a buzzer to indicate the error and the game terminates.

To apply Memory Techniques to any of these variations of the game, I would use the Phonetic Code System. For the integers, as the game proceeds, I would group them in twos, threes, or both. Then I would convert such a group to a word in my phonetic code peg list. I would link each word to the previous word using the Link System. For the game Simon or the game using the musical instrument, I would first assign to each button or key, a number from one to the number of buttons or keys used. Then I would apply the same methods.

The following is a game I've created that two or more can play. To play, the players take turns calling out., the name of a card of a typical card deck. A player is immediately disqualified if he or she calls out a card name that has already been called out during the game. The game continues in this way until there is but one player left, who is then the winner.

Upon the point whereas all card names have been called out, the player who goes next must announce to the other remaining players that there are no cards left. Then the entire game begins again with the remaining players, and beginning with the player making the announcement. These games continue in this way until there is but one player left. This player is then the winner.

To apply Memory Techniques to this game, the methods of *The Card Item* on page 69, and *Detecting Missing Cards* on page 70 are the techniques to use. I now leave it to you to figure out the rest of the details. At this point in the book, you have all the necessary knowledge to do so.

There are many such games to which children can learn to apply emory Techniques. There are some games made by Milton Bradley that bear the name *Memory*. There is at least one such game for every age. Teaching children such techniques will no doubt increase their chances of success in the future.

CONCENTRATION

A number peg system is quite useful when playing the board game Concentration. The game could consist of two or three players. There are many ways to construct and play this game. Here are some versions of the game that I've conceived.

Construct this first version as follows:

- Follow the directions as described in figure 2.

- Cut out 28 rectangular pieces of opaque stiff paper such as cardboard or index card paper. The length of the long side of each piece should be about 3/4 the width of one of the squares on the sheet in figure 2. The short side of each piece should be about half the height of one of the squares.

- Write on one side of the 28 pieces, the names of 14 items. That is, each name is to be written on two of the pieces and each piece is to have but one name only. Make sure that the writing is legible but cannot be seen through on the other side. I recommend that you use a pencil. Thus you can erase and change the names later if you wish to.

Set up the game as follows:

- Lay the sheet in figure 2 down so that the numbers are visible.

- Lay the 28 pieces onto the sheet with the names faced down.

-

Shuffle the pieces. Then without picking any of then up, slide each piece into a different square. Make sure that they are neat and that all numbers written on the sheet are visible. To play, each player takes turns turning over two of the pieces. If the names on them don't match, the player then turns them back over to the way they were, and it's the next player's turn. If they do match, the player then takes the two pieces then it's his or her turn to go again. The game is over when all the pieces have been taken. The player holding the most pieces is the winner. The advantage to have in this game is a good ability to remember the names you have seen and which number square each is on. To use the Peg System for this, the peg labels depict the numbers on the squares and the data placed into the pegs are the names on the pieces.

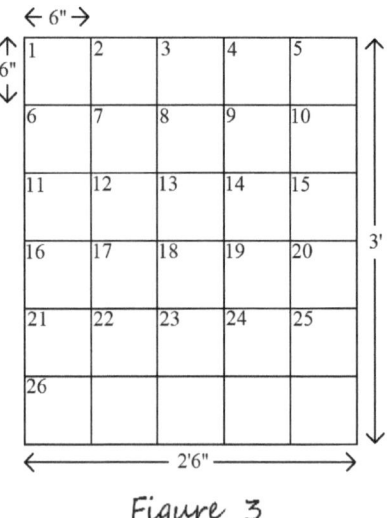

Figure 3

When playing this game with small children, it is probably better that the children do not turn over the pieces. To play in this way, an adult referee, who could also be one of the players, is to have the other players call out the numbers of the squares they choose. The referee is then the one to turn over the pieces and when appropriate, give pieces to a player. This principle applies to the other two games of this chapter that require a numbered sheet on which to lay pieces.

You could play this game alone. For this, you play in exactly the same way. However in this game, you also count the number of turns it takes to obtain all the pieces. You try to improve each time you play the game. This you do by trying to obtain all the pieces in a lower number of turns. This principle can apply to all other versions of Concentration.

You could make the game more difficult by doubling the quantities and numbers of everything. That is, you could make a larger sheet with twice the number of squares. You could have twice the number of pieces, etc. With this, you can have more players in the game as well.

The game Concentration can be played using a deck of cards and a large sheet of paper or cardboard (preferably cardboard) The sheet is to be a sized and marked such as that of figure 3 on page 95. You could make one or more of the sizes of the sheet a bit larger if you wish to.

To prepare to play, take the following steps:

- Take all jokers, spades, and clubs out of the card deck, thus leaving only the red suits, which are hearts and diamonds.

- Lay the sheet in figure 3 down with the numbers showing.

- Shuffle the deck then place each card faced down onto the sheet and into a different square. Make sure that they are all neat and that all numbers written on the sheet are visible.

This game is played exactly the same way as the previous version. The only difference pertains to what is considered a match. In this game a match is two cards of the same number. Examples are: two Jacks, two fives, or two aces.

You could double all the quantities and numbers of this version of the game as well. In this case, you would not take the spades and clubs out of the deck. In addition, a match in this case is two cards of the same number, and of the same color suit, which is either red or black.

To apply a memory technique to this version of the game, you use the Peg System in the same way as used in the previous version. However, the items placed into the pegs are to be card items as taught on page 69, which is within Chapter 21.

The following way to play concentration requires a small box index file set and a referee: First number the index places from 1 to, let's say, 40. Then on 40 cards, write the names of 20 items. Of course, each item appears on two of the cards.

To set the game up, the referee shuffles the cards then files them into the index places. To play, the prayers take turns calling out two of the 40 index numbers. As each player does this, the referee looks into the file then announces the items to each of the two numbers. If the items match, that player holds the two cards. If one or more of the two numbers contains no card, the player looses that turn. The game is over when there are no cards left and the player holding the most cards is the winner.

Although one could simply re-shuffle the cards to play again, one should occasionally change the items. This would help to keep the game interesting. Because of this, I recommend that one make the writing on the cards erasable. One could even have a number of sets of cards. One could also intermix these sets.

You could use instead of pieces of paper, a deck of playing cards. In this case, 52 numbered places are needed. Two cards of the same number and suit color (spade and club, or diamond and heart) are a match.

Another way to play requires but a pen, a paper and a referee. To set it up, the referee forms a numbered list of items. Each item appears twice in the list and all items are in random order. The referee should take suggestions for items from the participants, but must not reveal the order of items. The participants are never to see the list, however they are to know the length of it.

To play, the players take turns calling out two numbers of the list. The referee then announces to all, the item listed by each of the two numbers. If the items match, the referee puts the initials of that player by each of the two numbers then it is that players turn again. However, if they don't match or if the two already have initials, it is the next player's turn. The game is over when all the numbers have initials. The referee announces the player whose initials appear the most as the winner.

DICE AND DOMINOES

Two ideas I've come up with just before completing this book is to combine and apply Memory Techniques to Dice and Dominoes, and to create memory games with such. In this sub-chapter, I will cover all of this including four games I've invented so far. However, for those who don't know, in the next two paragraphs, I will explain what dice and dominoes are. Then in the following paragraph, I will cover ways of applying Memory Techniques to them.

First, of the word *dice,* there is a singular and plural form. The plural form is dice and the singular form is die. Therefore, dice is more than one die. A die is but a cube that is from 1/2 to 3/4 inches wide. A die has a number on each of its six surfaces. These numbers are the integers from 1 to 6. When tossing a die in a game, the players wait to see what number will be on the top surface when it lands and comes to a halt. For this entire sub-chapter, let's call this number the result of the toss. In most games involving dice, instead of one die, two dice are tossed together from one hand. In this case, the result of the toss would of course be two numbers. you can purchase dice in most stores that sell games, or in most small grocery stores. For some of the games in this chapter, I suggest that you obtain a pair of dice of colors different from each other.

A domino is a rectangular block that has~ a shape somewhat of a twin bed mattress. However, its length is only about two inches. One of its largest surfaces is its face on which there are two numbers on opposite sides with respect to the length. These numbers are the integers that range from 0 to 6, and there are 28 dominoes in a set. I refer to double six type dominoes, which are the most popular. This is the type of dominoes I use for almost all the lessons in this sub-chapter. In a set, the two number combination on each domino is unique and all possible combinations exist. You can purchase a set of dominoes in most stores that sell games.

typical dice

typical dominoes

One simple way to apply Memory Techniques to dice and dominoes involves the use of the Phonetic Code System. Of a pair of dice, a two digit number can depict the result of a toss. For instance, let's suppose that the result is a 3 and a 1. The number 31 or 13 can depict this result. Each of these two numbers consists of a 3 and a 1, and the order of the digits doesn't matter. Therefore, using the Phonetic Code, such words as *mat, tomb, meat, thumb,* and *mud* can indicate this result. Let's suppose that the result of a toss is a 2 and a 6. In this case, the number 26 or 62 applies, which then converts to such words as *notch, chain, wench* and *China.*

As I've said, the order of the two digits doesn't matter. However, It is to your advantage to always use the same order, whether it's the higher digit first or visa versa.

Of dominoes, you can apply the same methods. The two number combination on a domino would be handled in exactly the same way as the result of a toss of a pair of dice.

The first game requires a pair of dice, a sheet of lined paper and a p en or pencil. To play, each player takes turns tossing the pair of dice. the player tossing the dice must then recite in order the previous tosses that also produced that result. For example, it could be the twenty fifth toss in the game, and the result of that toss could have also occurred on the third, eight and seventeenth toss. Again, this is just an example. If the player's recital is incorrect, he or she loses a point. Each player's score is determined by the total number of tosses minus the number of points that player lost. The pen and paper are for recording the result- of each toss and the lost points of each player. I recommend, numerical listing for the toss results. For the lost points, I recommend the counting method of which you make small vertical parallel lines. Then on the fifth count, you put a line through the four lines. Then on the next count, begin the whole process again. As the player recites the previous tosses, the player who tossed just before him or her observes and updates the record, and tells all whether the recital is correct. To apply a memory technique to this game, you can use the Peg System. You could convert the result of a toss to the name of something then place it into a peg. Thus you would make in your mind, a numerical listing of the tosses.

Two or more can play this second game. This game requires a set of dominoes, a pair of dice, a pen and paper for recording scores, and a sheet as described in figure 2 on page 92.

Set up the game as follows:
- Lay the sheet down so that the numbers are visible.
- Lay all dominoes onto the sheet faced down then shuffle them.
- Without picking any of them up, slide each domino into a square so that there is a domino in each square. Make sure that they are neat and that all numbers written on the sheet are visible.

To play the game, the players take turns tossing the pair of dice. The player who tosses then turns over one of the dominoes so that all can see its face. When all have seen it, that player turns it back over onto its face. If the number combination on that domino is a zero and a zero (double blank), That player either loses a point or scores minus one point. If the number combination matches the result of the toss, that player scores a point. If this is a match, and the result of the toss is two of the same number (a double), that player must also do the following:

The player tosses one die. Then the player turns over one of the dominoes then turns it back over again exactly as in the previous procedure. If the face of that domino contains the combination of zero and the result of the toss, the player scores one extra point. If it isn't, the player scores no point for either toss.

Obviously the ability to quickly memorize the combination on the face of a domino as seen when it is turned over, along with the number of the square it's in is the advantage to have. For this, the Peg System is the memory system to use. In this case, the peg labels depict the numbers on the sheet. The data placed into the pegs depict the dominoes' combinations.

An additional rule one could add to the game pertains to the double blank. The rule is to increase by one the number of points a player loses for turning over the double blank each time it is turned over, in this case, a record should be kept and updated of the number of time that domino is turned over.

The following is another rule one could add: A player is to be docked a point for turning over a double domino that has already been turned over in the game. Of course this rule does not apply if it is a match to the result of the toss at hand. For this rule, a record of the double dominos turned over is necessary.

You could play this game alone. For this, you play in exactly the same way. However in this game, you also count the number of turns it takes to obtain a certain score. For instance, the score could be 100. You try to improve each time you play the game. This you do by trying to obtain the score in a lower number of turns.

To make the game even more challenging, you can play this game using Double Nine type dominoes. Double Nine dominoes have numbers on them ranging from 0 to 9 instead of from 0 to 6. In addition, there are 55 of these dominoes in a set instead of 28. To play this game using Double Nine dominoes, you must modify the sheet, the dice, and the rules. For better comprehension, I suggest that you read the rest of this chapter then review. In addition, I suggest that you draw your own diagrams as you study this subject matter.

For the sheet, you are to make a sheet that has 55 squares instead of 28. You are to number the squares from 1 to 55. It is possible to use two calendars fastened together. For this, you can use all the numbers from 1 to 30 on one of them and modify the numbers on the other using correction fluid and a pen or marker so that the count continues from 31 to 55.

As for the dice, I had to come up with a way in which the result of a toss can range from 1 and 1, to 9 and 9. After working on this problem for a while, I've come up with this answer. With the use of the method I'm about to describe, it is possible to obtain the desired result. Of this method, you put with each die a small coin. I recommend that you pair each die with such a coin close to the die's color. For example, I would pair a red die with a penny, and a die that is green or white, with a dime. Thus, it is easy to remember which coin goes with which die.

The way to use this set is like this: You toss the dice and the coins together from one hand. To derive one of the numbers, you add the result of one die to the result of its corresponding coin. The result of a coin that lands with its head up is **three**. The result of a coin that lands with its head down (tail up) is **zero**.

The following are some examples of results of tosses: A die landing with a two on top, with a coin landing with its head up, counts as **five**. A die landing with a six on top, with a coin landing with its tail up, counts as six. A die landing with a six on top, with a coin landing with its head up, counts as **nine**.

You can even use this system and dice in the first dice game on page Error: Reference source not found, to make that game more interesting.

If both dice are identical, you must also mark one die in order to tell one from the other, this is the reason I have said before that the dice should be of different colors from each other. The way I would mark one die is to add color into one or more dots of each of its six surfaces, using, for example, white correction fluid. That is, of course, if the dots were a dark color. Therefore, if the dots were a light color, I'd use a black pen instead.

This third game requires all the materials used in the previous game except the dice. It does require the sheet as described in figure 2 on page 92. The game also requires the top list on page 102.

Set up the game as follows:

- Lay the sheet down so that the numbers are visible.

- Lay all dominoes onto the sheet faced down then shuffle them.

- Without picking any of them up, slide each domino into a square so that there is a domino in each square. Make sure that they are neat and that all numbers written on the sheet are visible.

To play, the players take turns turning over the dominoes as one person, who could be one of the players, recites the top list on page 102 in order. When the person reciting calls out a line of the list (Notice that there are 28 lines total.), the player who's turn it is to go, is to turn over one of the dominoes. If that domino is a match to what was just called out, that player is to take that domino and the person reciting is to cross that line out. Therefore, I suggest that you copy the list and use the copy instead of that page. If it is not a match, that player, after all have seen its face, is to turn that domino back over as it was. Then the whole process repeats with the next line and the next player. This continues until all the lines have been called out. Then it all begins again at the top of the list. However, lines crossed out are always to be skipped. The game continues in the way until all dominoes have been taken and all lines are crossed out. Then the player holding the most dominoes is the winner.

Again, it is obvious that the ability to quickly memorize the combination on the face of a domino as seen when it is turned over, along with the number of the square it's in is the advantage to have. For this, the Peg System is the memory system to use. In this case, the peg labels depict the numbers on the sheet. The data placed into the pegs depict the dominos' combinations.

To play this game using Double Nine dominoes, you must modify the sheet, and use instead the bottom list on page 102. As for the sheet, you are to make a sheet that has 55 squares instead of 28. You are to number the squares from 1 to 55. It is possible to use two calendars fastened together. For this, you can use all the numbers from 1 to 30 on one of them and modify the numbers on the other using correction fluid and a pen or marker so that the count continues from 31 to 55.

This fourth game requires all the materials used in the previous game except the pen and list. Therefore, it requires the sheet as described in figure 2 on page 92.

Set up the game as follows:

- Lay all dominoes onto the sheet faced down then shuffle them.
- Lay all dominoes onto the sheet faced down then shuffle them.
- Without picking any of them up, slide each domino into a square so that there is a domino in each square. Make sure that they are neat and that all numbers written on the sheet are visible.

To play the game, each player takes his or her turn calling out a domino number combination, then turning over one of the dominoes. If ever a player turns over a domino that is a match to what he or she has just called out, the player is to take that domino. If it is not a match, when all have seen its face, the player is to turn that domino back over as it was.

In this game, the domino the first player turns over is that in square number 1. The domino the next player turns over is that in the next higher square, which is square number 2. The next player does the same process with the next higher square, which is of course square number 3, and so forth. Thus the dominoes are turned over in consecutive order with respect to the square numbers. The game continues in this way, up to the last square, which of course is number 28. Then the game continues with the lowest number square occupied by a domino. Any empty square is always to be skipped. This entire process continues on and on until all the dominoes have been taken. Then the player holding the most dominoes is the winner of the game.

Again, it is obvious that the ability to quickly memorize the combination on the face of a domino as seen when it is turned over, along with the number of the square it's in is the advantage to have. For this, the Peg System is the memory system to use. In this case, the peg labels depict the numbers on the sheet. The data placed into the pegs depict the dominoes' combinations.

To play this game using Double Nine dominoes, you must modify the sheet. To modify the sheet, you are to make a sheet that has 55 squares instead of 28. You are to number the squares from 1 to 55. It is possible to use two calendars fastened together. For this, you can use all the numbers from 1 to 30 on one of them and modify the numbers on the other using correction fluid and a pen or marker so that the count continues from 31 to 55.

DOUBLE SIX DOMINO LIST

0,0	1,1	2,3	3,6
0,1	1,2	2,4	4,4
0,2	1,3	2,5	4,5
0,3	1,4	2,6	4,6
0,4	1,5	3,3	5,5
0,5	1,6	3,4	5,6
0,6	2,2	3,5	6,6

DOUBLE NINE DOMINO LIST

0,0	1,5	3,4	5,7
0,1	1,6	3,5	5,8
0,2	1,7	3,6	5,9
0,3	1,8	3,7	6,6
0,4	1,9	3,8	6,7
0,5	2,2	3,9	6,8
0,6	2,3	4,4	6,9
0,7	2,4	4,5	7,7
0,8	2,5	4,6	7,8
0,9	2,6	4,7	7,9
1.1	2,7	4,8	8,8
1,2	2,8	4,9	8,9
1,3	2,9	5,5	9,9
1,4	3,3	5,6	

CHAPTER 25

MISCELLANEOUS SYSTEMS

There are many such systems that I am sure you know of. One that I would bet that you know is: *Thirty days has September, April June and November.* It is sometimes possible for you to invent such a phrase to assist is memorizing certain information.

Another example of such a phrase, I learned in an electronics course I had taken. It pertains to the following rule:

Voltage leads current in an inductive circuit, where as current leads voltage in a capacitive circuit.

Now, all the students and I already knew well, that C depicts capacitance, E depicts voltage, I depicts current, and L depicts inductance. They are popular symbols in electronics. To memorize the rule above, we were taught the phrase, *ELI the ICE man.*

Notice that in *ELI,* L (inductive) is the center letter and E is before I (voltage leads current). Now compare all of this with *ICE.*

ACROSTICS

An acrostic is a sentence of which the first letter of each word, and the order of these letters, is the same as that of a series of letters or another series of words to memorize. This is a memory system you probably have used yourself. Anyone who is familiar with music knows of the acrostic: *Every Good Boy Does Fine.*

Let me tell you about an acrostic I learned to help memorize resistor color coding. Anyone who has seen the inside of any electronic device, such as a radio, has seen resistors. Resistors are those small brown cylindrical objects with the colored rings painted around them, inside electronic devices such as radios. The color of such a ring sometimes depicts a certain digit.

The digit assignments of the colors are:

    0. black
    1. brown
    2. red
    4. orange
    5. yellow
    6. green
    7. blue
    8. violet
    9. gray
    0.1. white

The acrostic we learned to help memorize this is: **Bad Boys Rob Our Young Girls But Violet Gives Willingly.** Notice that the first letters of these words are the same as the first letters of the colors in the list, and in the same order.

My point is that you can create such sentences to help memorize certain information. If you want to know what the rest of the coding entails, read the next paragraph. If not, skip it.

There are three or four rings on a resistor. To avoid mistaking the first ring for the last, or visa versa, the first ring is closer to its end than the last ring is to the other. The rings depict the amount of ohms of the resistor. Ohms is the measurement of electrical resistance, just as degrees is the measurement of temperature. The first ring depicts the first digit. The second ring depicts the second digit. The third ring depicts the number of zeros to follow the two digits. A third ring that is gold Depicts 1/10 of the number indicated by the two digits. A silver third ring depicts 1/100 of it. A silver fourth ring depicts a 10% tolerance of the so indicated resistance. A gold fourth ring depicts 5% tolerance. The absence of the fourth ring depicts 20% tolerance. Again, to understand any such information better, draw your own diagram and mark it accordingly.

One could use an acrostic with the Phonetic Code System to memorize a number. I find this method very effective. For numbers a person wants to memorize for a long time, I feel that this is the best system to use.

For an example, let's apply it to the new girls telephone number on page 38. Again, the number is 718 615 2894. First, we must choose corresponding phonetic code letters. Choosing such letters at random, I've derived the following:

G T F Sh D L N F B R

I myself can already see a potential sentence. I would need to insert eight blanks. Doing so, I derive.

I G T F O I SH I D A W L A N F B O R

The acrostic I've thought of is:

I GOT TO FIND OUT IF SHE IS DEPRESSED AND WOULD LIKE A NICE FANCY BOUQUET OF ROSES.

Notice that the first letter of each word corresponds to the series of letters I've just formed. Thus, I've changed the number into a sentence that I can easily imagine and recall. Try this with any such number. Of course it may take a little time and thinking to apply. Nevertheless it pays off.

ACRONYMS

Another useful system is an acronym. An acronym is a word formed from the first letters of other words. One acronym I think of immediately is *WASPLEG*. This is part of the title of the book, *Waspleg and other mnemonics*. This book, and others, contains many such miscellaneous systems for many subjects. In the word **WASPLEG,** W is for wrath. A is for avarice. S is for sloth. P is for pride. L is for lust. E is for envy, and G is for gluttony. These are the well-known *Seven Deadly Sins.*

You can use something similar to an acronym to memorize numbers, with the use of the Phonetic Code. It can also be done with the use of the telephone dial number/letter combinations. Businesses use such a system to aid customers in remembering their phone numbers. They have appeared in many advertisements.

CHAPTER 26

SCHOOL & TECHNICAL SUBJECTS

Here, I will cover a few applications since at this point, you have all the necessary knowledge to handle these subjects. Nevertheless, I will state some examples.

SPELLING

I've found that spelling problems differ, and that each type of problem could be handled in different ways. Examples of different types of problems are:

1. Knowing whether to place two of a letter together, or the letter alone. For example, which is correct, proceedure or procedure.

2. Uncertainty of the correct vowel to place in a particular part of a word. For example, which spelling is correct, attendance or attendence.

3. Which spelling is correct for either of two words that sound the same or similar. For example, which word depicts office supplies, stationery or stationary.

4. Uncertainty whether to join two words as one or to have them separate, for instance, which word depicts completion, all ready or already.

5. Knowing immediately when you have spelled a word incorrect.

Of course, you must first learn spelling rules well. Provided you have, you can begin to use Mnemonics to assist you in these problems. I will address some of these problems.

For problems 1, 2, and 4, in most cases, you can solve your problem by memorizing the letters of the word in their proper order. It is even more effective to learn to do it both backwards and forwards. For this, you could even use mnemonics. For instance, you could apply the Link System or the Story Method to a series of items that depict the letters. Of course, I would use the items in my alphabet list on page 37. For an example, take the word **ERYTHROBLASTOSIS**. The Link System applies to this word as follows:

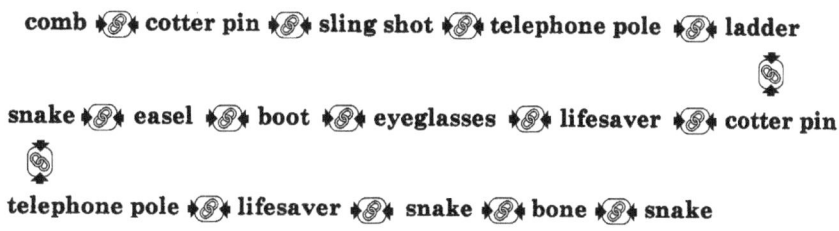

Notice that this is the same notation of depicting linking, as taught on page 18. Also, as I implied, these items were taken from my alphabet list on page 37. For instance, the first item of the series (comb) depicts the letter E. The next item (cotter pin) depicts R. The next (sling shot) depicts Y, and so forth. When applying the Link System in this way, I advise that you place at the beginning of the series, an image depicting the word (See *Words and Names* on page 40.). With this additional image, this method is a solution for problem 3 as well. There is more you can do with this idea. For one, it is not necessary that the word be divided into portions of only one letter each. Sometimes, some portions of a word could be whole syllables and whole words. For example, the word above could be divided as follows:

E R Y THROB LAST O S I S

As you can see, I've found within it the words *throb* and *last.* Applying the Link System to this series, I derive:

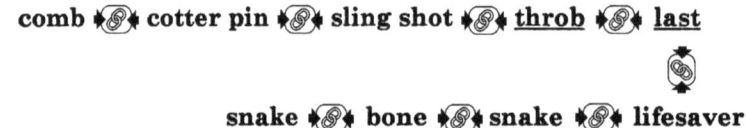

Obviously, one advantage is that this series is much shorter than the series above. When recalling the mental scenes you Would create for this series, you would know the meaning and purpose of each mental scene simply because of your common sense. For instance, consider this: Since you are the person who creates the mental scene, upon your recalling it, you would of course know the meaning and purpose of every element in it. Therefore, from this, you would derive the correct spelling of the word.

Now that I think of it, you can use for spelling certain systems designed for memorizing mathematical formulas. One that applies well for this is the second advanced memory system that begins on page 125. That memory system is for memorizing a series of characters. The spelling of a word is nothing more than that. Therefore, that memory system can apply to spelling as well.

However, I would slightly modify that system when applying it to spelling. For this alteration, I would assign all alphabet letters from A to Z the numbers 01 to 26 instead of from 11 to 36. In this case, all other number assignments are to be used as blanks. Just keep in mind that these changes apply to the system only for spelling. Provided you know well the place numbering of every alphabet letter, this method should work well. Of course, this is also a solution for problems 1, 2, and 4. Again, I advise that you place at the beginning of the word series, an image depicting the word. Thus, this method is a solution for problem 3 as well.

For problem 5, you could periodically evaluate your spelling using a dictionary or thesaurus. For this, there are also electronic dictionaries, thesauruses, and spelling checkers on the market. The latest word processors can be of great help in solving this problem. Most of these word processors are equipped with spelling checkers. If you type a letter or document into such a word processor, you could then activate its spelling checker. The spelling checker will go through the document stopping and alerting you to words misspelled. As it stops on a word, it lets you correct its spelling. For most words, the spelling checker will also show you its correct spelling. Therefore, you can use such a word processor as an instrument to find the words you spell wrong. However, there can be some problems with this. For instance, let's suppose that a word in the document is not the correct spelling for what you intend it to mean. The spelling checker will not stop on it if it's the correct spelling for another meaning. Such a word is called a homonym.

One solution for problems 2. and 3. is to try to see one or more smaller words in the word. When you see such a word in it, make an association of the word and the meaning of the word in question. For example, in the word attendance, I see the word *dance* in it (atten*dance*). To remember the correct spelling for this word, imagine that the word pertains to attending a dance. You can form mental scenes for this as well. For instance, you could imagine that men are dancing with ladies wearing roll books *(Roll book* is my image for the word attendance).

For other examples, especially for problem 3, to cure the problem of spelling the word piece, one could associate it with a piece of pie. For the word peace, one could associate it with a fighter ace pilot who wants peace.

If you cannot see a smaller word in the word in question, try to find the name of something that rhymes with the part of the word you are unsure of. Take for example the words stationary and stationery as shown in problem 3. The difference between them is within the last three letters of each. To remember that *stationary* means motionless or standing, you could make the association of stationary and fairy. For this, you could imagine a stationary fairy, that cannot move because she cannot lift her feet off the ground. For *stationery,* which means *office supplies,* you could imagine that in a store that sells stationery the salesman rides around in the store in a ferry boat. Although the spelling of both fairy and ferry are inaccurate for these examples they will work because of their sounds.

Another way of dealing with spelling problems 1, 2, and 3 is to associate a word with a smaller related word one already knows how to spell. I used to have difficulty with the word different. To cure it, I associated it with the word differ. It also helps to form sentences to associate with difficult words. For the word different, one can also use the statement: It differs if it's different.

Another aid for problems 1,2, and 3 is to exaggerate the pronunciation of a word to sound more like its correct spelling.

VOCABULARY AND LANGUAGE

A language is but a code. Therefore, I would handle it as such. To adequately learn the lessons of this chapter, it is essential to know the subject matter in Chapter 12, which begins on page 40.

To memorize the meaning of a word, simply form a scene that involves the images depicting the word and its meaning. I would also add to such a scene, an image that indicates that the scene is for memorizing a vocabulary word. In the examples here, I use the image of *dictionary* for this purpose.

For example, the word sagacious means *of good judgment.* To apply this technique, you can imagine, for instants, a Japanese geisha woman wearing a kimono made of loose dictionary pages. Everything she touches in the courtroom begins to sag. She is a judge and she is always extolled for being a good one.

The word extol means *praise highly.* To apply it to this, You could imagine a huge egg using a bathroom stall and reading a gigantic dictionary. People are extolling the egg for learning how to read and use the stall.

The word surreptitious means underhanded and sly. In me, this definition brings to mind the image of a sneaky looking mugger. The sound of the word surreptitious brings to my mind the image of tissues saturated with maple syrup. To apply the system, I might imagine that this mugger, just before he attempts to carry out a crime, wipes his face with such tissues. With his face so covered with the syrup, you can't see what he looks like. To scare him off, just show him a dictionary. He can't read and the thought of trying to scares him.

To apply this to a word of another language, my method is to ssociate the word, the meaning, and the language with one another. Notice that I've simply replaced the image for *vocabulary* with one for *language.* I include this third image for the same reason that I do for vocabulary words. For a language, another reason is to enable the application of the system to more than one language concurrently. My image for the Spanish language is that of a Mexican sombrero. For French, is that of the Eiffel Tower.

For example, the Spanish word for thing is *cosa*. For this word, one could imagine the *Thing* (see the forth paragraph of Chapter 12 which is on page 40) trying to swim in an ocean that consists of tiny twirling colorful sombreros instead of water. However, he keeps getting washed back onto the coast. He is complaining about it and having a temper tantrum.

The French word for ant is *fourmi*. It's pronounced "foomee". To me, it sounds close to *foamy*. To apply; I might imagine giant ants that continuously regurgitate sweet smelling colorful foam. The ants are constructing an ant hill with this foam. The hill will have the shape of the Eiffel Tower. The French word for slow is *lent.* For this word, one imagines, for instance, that in the vicinity of the Eiffel Tower, everything and everyone moves very slowly. The reason is that the French police use *lent* to slow down all the motorists and pedestrians. To do this, they drop large amounts of this lent on the streets and sidewalks. These police must always carry enormous quantities of this *lent* around with them. For anyone who even talks fast, if one of these cops witnesses it, he will immediately stuff some of this *lent* into the person's mouth.

The Spanish word for tree is *albol*. To me, this sounds close to *oil bowl*. It also sounds like *elbow*. However, I don't want to confuse it with *coda*, which is the Spanish equivalent of *elbow*. One must use ones own judgment in these matters. For this, I might imagine that I'm in a forest. The trees in this forest grow sombreros instead of leaves. It is fall. Therefore, sombreros are falling everywhere. Such a place is where Mexican people come to obtain such hats. I have the task of carrying around a gigantic metal bowl of strong smelling oil. I must rub this oil on the trees. The trees themselves direct me where to rub the stuff on them.

Recall of the meaning of the foreign word is simple enough. For this, one thinks of what scene it is in which the foreign word's image and the image depicting the language is together. The recall of the foreign equivalent of a word is similar. For this, think of what scene is in which the word's image is with the image depicting the language. For either one of these actions applied to the same image association, the same scene would come to mind.

As in all codes, you should be careful of your choice of backgrounds of your imaginary scenes. Never choose a background that pertains to the image common in all the scenes. Otherwise, the background and surroundings in all the scenes would be the same, which can cause confusion. In this chapter, the images common are those that depict the language, such as *sombrero* and *Eiffel Tower*. Therefore, my scene for the French word for slow, which is the Eiffel Tower, is a bad choice. Instead, for each scene, choose a background that pertains to one of the other two images. Thus, all of your scenes would be of different places, and this would prevent confusion.

Another way to avoid this problem is to be careful of your choice of images depicting the languages. For this, choose items that are not stationary and unique such as the Eiffel Tower. Such items should be items that could be found anywhere. For *French,* one choice of such an image could be that of a Can Can girl.

The techniques of this chapter are more effective if you apply a large number of words at a time, such as 100. In addition, you should practice recalling the definitions of the words in random order. When you know them well, repeat the process with new words, and so forth. If you find 100 to be too easy, increase the number of words. This practice also applies to any other type of code. When you reach the topic of natural associations in Chapter 28, you will find more about language.

HISTORY AND GOVERNMENT

A person can certainly use the basic techniques to aid in memorizing quite a variety of historical facts. For example, lets suppose that I want to memorize: The first shipment of slaves from Africa arrived in America in 1619. For this, I might imagine that slaves are riding in a ship. They are playing tubas' made of porcelain (1619 is *dish tuba*) as New Years Eve horns and hats (my image for *year)* dance. The hats and horns often accidentally hit the tubas causing them to break. The hat and horns are kicking around the fragments from the tubas. Any additional information is then linked to this scene.

Information in a particular order, such as the articles and amendments of the Constitution, is best applied using the Linking From Pegs technique. To explain, I will apply it to the 18th amendment. It went into effect in 1917 and prohibited the sale and manufacture of liquor. For this, I might imagine the following scene:

Doves (peg 18) are mending (amendment) their feathers using strong smelling whiskey and running from a cop because whiskey is illegal. Another scene follows in which the largest of the doves has been caught. It is in jail and it's sharing a huge smelly rotten egg (917 is *bad egg* and the first digit isn't necessary.) with a New Years Eve hat and horn. Again, additional information would then be linked to this last scene. Also, apply the lessons of Chapter 4.

For more applications on school subjects, I recommend the book, *Super Memory - Super Student.*

TYPING

In this day and age, because of computer technology, any technique that helps in the development of typing skill is valuable. I myself wanted to learn to type efficiently, so I looked to mnemonics as an aid. In the process, I've formed a system I've found quite effective for the task.

Speed and accuracy are the most important factors in typing skill. Accuracy in this case is the ratio of the number of correct keys pressed to the total number pressed. Therefore, the fewer errors in keys pressed that a person makes in typing, the more accurate that person is in typing. The typing speed of a person is simply the number of words per minute that person can type.

For speed and accuracy, memorizing the relative location of each alphabet letter on the keyboard is quite significant. Also for this, memorizing the fingering scheme is just as important. The only other factor is practice. To become an efficient typist one must have the ability to type without errors without looking at the keys. This calls for a good memorization of the keyboard.

This memory system would definitely assist in mentally establishing both alphabet key locations and fingering. As of many of the techniques throughout this book, this system is merely a way of quickly memorizing all the details. Then through practice, such details can become so firmly established in mind that the memory techniques applied would no longer be necessary for any recall. This is basically the way to use this memory system.

Before I get into the memory system, I will now describe the keyboard letters and fingering to which you are to apply the system.

Figure 4 on page 112 depicts the relative positions of all alphabet keys, along with the fingering. I omitted almost all other keys because for these lessons, they are unnecessary. One key has no character on it because this character varies with different - models and makes of keyboards. Notice that I've divided the keyboard into eight sections, of which for the sake of these lessons, I numbered along the top. As the diagram shows, each of the fingers (except the thumbs) is to be used in but one particular section only. The key in each section that has the heavy outlining is that on which the finger of that section is to be placed when inactive.

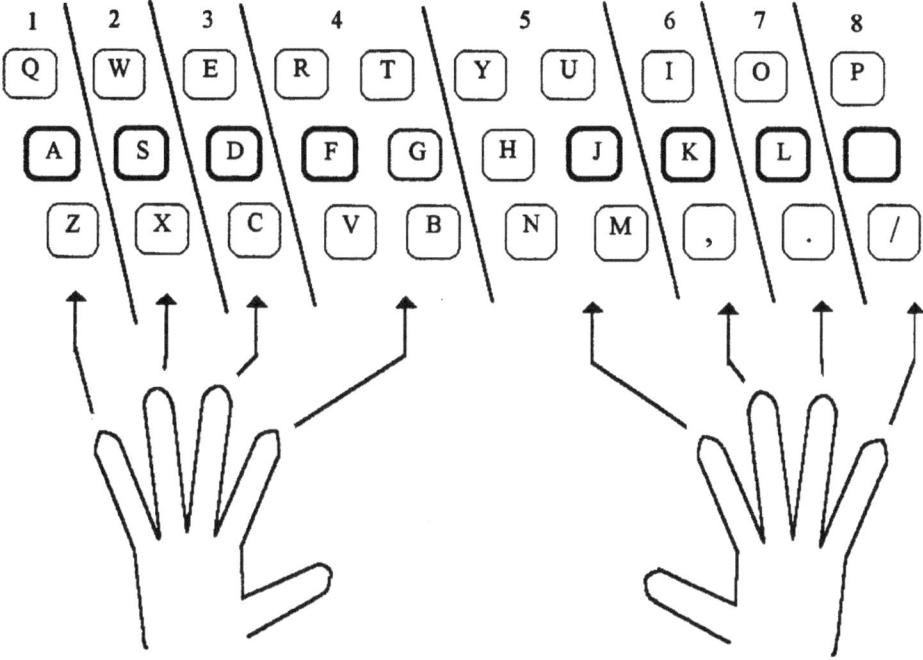

Figure 4

One easy way to memorize all of this is to apply the Loci System to each finger of the sections. For this, you associate each of your own fingers with the letters of that finger's section. Again, I derive letter images from my alphabet list on page 37.

For an example of how I could associate my leftmost finger (my left little finger) with the three letters in its section (Q, A, and Z), I could do the following:

I imagine that this particular finger contains a paintbrush (easel for A) that partially ejects out when I'm ready to use it. I use this brush to turn the knobs on my stereo or television (radio knob for Q). I also use it to paint my fire escape (Z) many pretty colors.

This next example depicts these principles as applied to my next finger, which is that of section 2. To associate this finger with its letters (W, S, and X), I could imagine that from the tip of this finger a snake (S) has grown. This snake wears a tuxedo (W), has arms and holds a large pair of scissors (X). Therefore, I often use this finger for cutting of which the snake does all the work.

For another example, to associate the next finger with its letters (E< D< and C) I might imagine a bow (D) mounted on the tip of this finger. I use this bow to shoot combs at the moon.

Notice that of the three examples I've just used, I've placed most emphasis on the letters the fingers are on when neutral. In the examples, these letters are A, S, and D. Notice in figure 4 that these letters have heavy outlines.

However, I did see a problem with the forth and fifth sections. Of any one of these sections, its finger operates six keys instead of three. I found it awkward to associate one finger with as much as six letters. As an alternative, for these two sections, I do the following.

For the fourth section, I associate the finger with the letters on the left (R, F, and V), and I associate the letters of the right (T, G, and B) with the left thumb.

I do almost the same with the fifth section. For this section, I associate its finger with the letters on the right (U, J, and M) and the right thumb with the left letters (Y, H, and N)

Now I will demonstrate the use of all these associations to recall the location of a certain letter, and without looking at the keyboard. First I must mention that with a little familiarity with the keyboard, remembering the position (top, middle, or bottom) of a key in a certain section is no problem for most people.

To find and hit the W key, I would first think of the that the tuxedo tail (W). From this, I would recall the tuxedo worn by the snake that is an extension of the finger that's next to the leftmost finger. I would then move this finger from its present (neutral) position to the key above that and hit it.

To find and strike the C key, I would think of the moon (C). This would bring to mind, the finger of the third section. I would then move this finger from its neural position to the key below, and strike that key.

As for any letter associated with the thumb, I do likewise, except that I use the finger next to that thump to strike the key, instead of the thump.

With the use of this system, you can improve your typing skill with or without a keyboard. With a typewriter or computer, you can practice by monitoring the results on the paper or viewing screen as you type. With this, the only time necessary to look at the keyboard is to initially position your fingers.

You could work on your typing skill anytime you are unoccupied. To practice using this method, you simply imagine your fingers striking the keys when reading or listening to someone talk. For instance, you could do this while riding on a train or bus and reading the advertisements. There are many other situations that provide this sort of opportunity.

As you work on your typing skill using any of these methods, you would soon find yourself hitting the correct keys without the need to think of any of the associations you had formed. Thus, the memory system would have served its purpose and would no longer be needed. When this occurs, you should continue to improve your speed. It helps immensely to practice anticipating the next key location and finger as you strike a particular key. With this, you would soon find yourself positioning your fingers more quickly and would type more quickly. Also to improve speed, work to become accustomed to the key sequences of whole words.

FOR THE COMPUTER TECH

This sub-chapter is written particularly for personnel in the computer technical field. To comprehend it, it is necessary to know well the first Morse Code System of Chapter 23 (on page 83). One must also know about Binary and Octal numbers on page 75. To better comprehend the lessons here, you should draw your own diagrams as you study them.

Computers use the Binary Number System for the following reason: A computer is but a mass of a great multitude of minute relays and a few electrical switches (A relay is an electrical switch controllable remotely by one or more other switches or relays.). Many of these relays and switches work together in chain reactions (such as switches that control relays, that control other relays, that control other relays, etc.). These chain reactions are all in a precise predetermined order. The end result is an output such as a word processor, video game, or whatever the computer is programmed to do.

Memory circuits inside the computer consist of many rows of this type of relays. Of such a row, some relays are on and some are off, set to a particular combination by the input. A specific combination could depict a particular number, letter or symbol, instruction or status code. Of course, a binary number could depict such a combination. For this, a 1 depicts an "on" state in the series, and a 0 depicts an "off" state in it.

The Octal Number System is also used in such applications, and in this book, for two reasons. For one, like our customary Decimal Number System (base ten system), an octal number consists of fewer digits than its binary equivalent. This is helpful in situations of which a large width (number of digits), as in most binary numbers, is undesirable. The other reason is that for both man and machine, converting from binary to octal, or visa versa, is much easier than converting from binary to decimal or visa versa.

One way to apply a memory technique to memorizing a binary number is simple and practical. You could convert the binary number to octal, then apply the result to the Phonetic Code System. Then of course you form the appropriate mental scenes for recall of the words. To recall the binary number, you recall the octal number from the phonetic code words and scenes you would have formed, then convert it back to binary. It's all that simple. Again, to learn about binary and octal numbers, refer to *Binary and Octal Numbers* on page 75.

There is more you could add to this method. For an example, here is a way to increase flexibility by changing some of the phonetic code rules when applying it to an octal number. An octal number does not have any digits that are 8 or 9. Therefore, the phonetic code letters F, V, P, and B would normally not be used. However, you could add these four letters to the group of phonetic code blanks (W, H, Y, vowels and spaces). This provides more flexibility in forming phonetic code words and/or sentences. Again, this sort of modification applies only to octal numbers. There are other possible variations of this ideal. For instance, instead of using F, V, P, and B as blanks, any of them can be used to depict other characters such as the comma, period, or dash.

Another way to apply mnemonics to binary numbers is to adapt the first Morse Code Memory System. The lessons of this system begin on page 83. To do this, simply apply the number to it as if each 1 were a dot and each 0 were a dash. In staying consistent with that system, the 7th and 8th digits each convert to either 7 or 8, and the 9th and 10th each convert to either 9 or 0. At this point, I suggest that you review the lessons of that Morse Code System, then review this paragraph.

Some applications of the lessons here are internal dip switch settings, jumper settings, and binary status codes.

To begin, let's take the following binary number:

1 0 0 1 0 1 0 1 1 1 0 1 0 1 1 1 .

Applying that system to the first ten digits, I've derive the words:

tin, rum, jail, fog, popeye

To memorize such a series of words, you can of course apply it to the Link System or the Story Method. You could even use the Phonetic Code to convert the number to a sentence. When using any of these techniques, make sure that the first image is that of an item that indicates the purpose of the binary number.

For some applications, it isn't necessary to keep the digits in groups of two. For instance, you could convert the digits instead to:

thinner, match, yellow-fog, popeye

In a case such as this, when converting the words back to digits, you must re-group the digits back into twos.

At this point, you may wonder what to do about the digits to the right of the 10th digit. Well, I simply begin again. That is, I convert the 11th and 12th each to either 1 or 2, and so on.

In some computer applications, a person is concerned with only certain digits in such a number. Such digits are usually separated into pairs and this system works quite well for this. For instance, suppose that you want to memorize only what the 5th and 6th characters are of the number above. In this case, only one word is necessary. A word that applies in this case is *shell*. Obviously the word shell can only be for the 5th and 6th digits and that the digits are 01. For another example, the word *rum* can only depict that the 3rd and 4th digits are 01. If, for example, the third and forth digits were 11 instead, the appropriate word would be *mummy*.

Let's suppose that the above number depicts the combination set in a certain row of relays in a computer, as a status code. The 5th and 6th digits of the number, when they are 01, indicate that the printer is active. To memorize this, simply associate *printer* with *shell*. Suppose that if the same digits changed to 11, it indicates that the disk drive is now active instead. For this, simply associate *disk drive* with *lily*. With this system, you can easily memorize all such aspects of all the digits.

There is one problem with this, and it is for digits after the 10th. I solve this problem by converting such digits to a word of which the first letter is a phonetic code blank. For example, for the 13th and 14th digits of the number above, I might convert them to *worm* instead of, for instance, *ram*. Of course, the w denotes that the places of these digits are both 10 higher than the values indicated by the rm.

This system also works if of such a pair, the left digit's place is of an even number. Let's suppose that we were considering the 6th and 7th digits. Of the number above they are 10. For this, a word you can apply is *shack*. If they were 01 instead, a word that would fit is *cash*.

There is a problem with this when it comes to identical digits. Take for instance *mummy*. In this case, there is no way to tell whether the digits are the 2nd and 3rd, or the 3rd and 4th. I solve this by imagining the mummy upside down if it's the 2nd and 3rd digits, and right side up if it's the 3rd and 4th. Therefore the upside down mummy indicates that the 2nd and 3rd digits are 00, and an upside down nun indicates that these digits are 11. Of course, this solution is not necessary for digits that are different from each other.

To apply an odd number of digits, I pair up all the left most digits, leaving one alone. If you look, you would see that such is the case with some letters of the first Morse Code systems of Chapter 23 on page 83.

CHAPTER 27

SPEECHES, BOOKS & STUDYING

I suggest that when reading anything, for better comprehension, it's good to avoid reading too much at a time. Therefore, its better to read only a comfortable portion at a time, each with a comfortable interval of rest and reflexion on the portion just read.

For a speech, it's usually necessary to memorize only the subjects you will cover, the significant details, and the sequence in which to cover each. In most cases, it is necessary only that the speaker make sure that he or she does not forget significant details. The Link or Peg System would be quite sufficient for this purpose. In applying such techniques, your first step would be to assign a key image for each significant detail. Although you could memorize a speech word for word using the same systems, This would render the speech very rigid and unnatural in its sound.

I recommend that you first organize the speech on paper, then memorize it using the techniques. You can apply all of this to other incidents such as speaking to an employer or customer. It is also applicable to jokes.

Consider this. As you probably know, it is uncomfortable for the eyes to remain fixed on one point for an extensive length of time. Therefore, a desire to stop looking at the spot would result. It is therefore logical that a person giving a speech should move around.

The application to books is similar. Of course, you can memorize a book word for word. A good way to do this is to use the Link from Pegs technique, with the pegs depicting the pages, and the links depicting the words. However, as I said for speeches, I don't recommend this for reading, and for the same reasons.

As I read, for each inch of text, I make sure that I mentally register the words I've just seen. That is, for each inch I think of the thought these words depict. Thus, I convert the words into thoughts. To read fast, you must learn to make such thoughts come to mind rapidly. The lessons of *Detecting Missing Cards* in Chapter 21 provides a good exercise for this. In these lessons, I've stated that it is good practice to learn to recall mentally the card items in rapid succession. The practice of recalling ideas and thoughts in rapid succession is a very good exercise for reading. The faster you can convert words into ideas, the faster and more comprehensively you can read. Another similar exercise for this is in the first two paragraphs of Chapter 30, which is on page 132. As I finished reading a sentence, I combine the thoughts into an idea. Then as I complete a paragraph, I combine the ideas, and so forth. It is equally good to learn to do these tasks rapidly.

As you read, pay attention to punctuation symbols. This will help to avoid misunderstandings. This applies especially to periods and commas. Removing a comma or period from a sentence can completely change its meaning. Therefore, if you miss a comma or period while reading a sentence, you may interpret it wrong. Think about it. Has this ever happened to you? Also, commas and periods are small and can be difficult to spot so look for them when reading.

I've found that when reading, it is best that you do not try to maintain a uniform speed. The reason is that some words are less difficult to read than others, therefore, can be read more quickly than others. It is not necessary to read each word in the same amount of time. Trying to maintain a uniform speed would cause errors if reading too quickly. It would cause unnecessary lag if reading too slowly. Therefore, read difficult words more slowly and read easier more obvious words more quickly. This rule applies especially to large words of which attention to detail is often important.

For reading to study, it is better to first examine the material's organization and structure. Therefore, you should look at the table of contents and the summary in the back of the book. Also, you should look at the summery at the end of the chapter and the questions. Thus, you would know what to expect when reading. You should also form questions you hope to have answered by the material. Also, one should determine what one wants to get out of the study period. It also helps to set an amount to cover for a particular study period.

It is natural for you to have a great tendency to. want to know the usefulness of subject matter you study. If you can't find such answers, you may tend to lose interest in the subject matter. This loss of interest severely impairs your study effectiveness. Therefore, you should try to find such answers if it's possible. For cases of which you can't, you must learn to suppress the desire for such answers. That is, you must learn not to concern yourself with the usefulness of the subject matter. Just learn the subject matter regardless.

To find such answers, it helps to try to think of practical examples to which the subject matter applies. This also improves your comprehension. If the subject matter does provide examples, you should still try to think of some of your own.

You may become discouraged from trying to learn subject matter you find difficult. For this, it helps not to think of such subject matter as difficult to learn. Instead, think of it as subject matter that only requires more time to learn.

As I've stated in the beginning, you can recall more easily, information that makes sense to you. This applies to reading as well. As you read, continue as long as the material you are reading is making sense to you. If during your reading, it ceases to make sense, a review may help. If not, you should research to obtain the information needed to understand the subject matter. However, if the reading material is poorly organized, a look ahead just might help.

You should also try to see whether you can interpret a passage of subject matter in more than one way. If you find that you can, you should then try to find the correct interpretation. The ability to interpret such a passage in different ways is a flaw made by the author. This you will most likely encounter many times. To help to avoid this problem, it is good to learn from more than one book.

I've found it quite helpful to anticipate the details of the subject matter I am to learn. For instance, before lessons on data base programs, I might derive my own ideas as best I could, of how data base programs work. In doing this, I put myself into a thinking mode for the lessons beforehand. Besides, I might derive some correct answers to my own questions. I also develop my sense of reasoning and imagination. During or after the lessons, I compare my ideas with what I learned from the lessons.

One should always compare similar or coexisting subjects or details. In doing this, you exercise your judgment and find more associations. The more associations, the better. In addition, after working out a problem, you should always compare the initial problem with the result.

One good way to test and improve your comprehension of a passage of reading material is to re-phrase it. If you can, you can safely say that you comprehend.

You should quickly skim over, if not bypass, material you already know. Thus, you reduce time waste. Highlighting reading material is not such a good idea. The only reason for highlighting I find justifiable is to emphasize certain text for someone else to see. When you highlight, you relay a message to the brain. The message is:

```
Because this information is highlighted, it is easy to find
in the book. Therefore, it is not so necessary to later
recall this data. Therefore it needs no attention as to its
storage.
```

Therefore, the brain would give the information no emphasis or storage care. Because of this, you would have more difficulty recalling this information. Besides, highlighting mars the book. However, I do recommend one system of highlighting. With this system, you do not highlight. You underline or circle with a soft pencil line. Thus, you make a mark you can easily erase without marring the book. When you are certain that you know a passage of information so marked, you then erase the marking. This would, of course, aid in skimming over information you already know.

Also, don't mark off a passage of information because you assume the information is important. Mark it off because you don't fully understand it. I mention this because your teacher may have different ideas of what is important. This would become clear by his or her tests. Therefore, it is also a good idea to get to know the teacher. Thus you can find out what the teacher thinks is important.

It is usually better to draw your own diagrams as you study subject matter of which diagrams can possibly be of help. This is so, even if the subject matter already provides such diagrams. You would, of course, understand diagrams you create yourself much better.

To apply mnemonics to studying, it is best to form a strategy before you begin. That is, you first decide exactly what techniques to use and how to use them. For this, you could use the techniques and organization that I covered at the beginning of this chapter for speeches. However, I would apply artificial associations only to the significant details of the subject matter. For the images and scenes, you should decide on such details as backgrounds for mental scenes and what to place in them. To use Memory Techniques effectively for studying, all of this should be well planned and organized. One book that specialized in this topic is *Memory Power For Exams*.

Since the mind records information in associations, and the more the better, it is logical to use this concept when studying. For instance, you could use Multiple Branching (on page 31) to link ideas and details. Fo each idea or detail, create a mental icon (see Words and Names on pag 58) of it. These icons, you are to link together into branches using Multiple Branching. Of course, you would start with the main topic then have its sub-topics branch off of it. Of each of these sub-topics, its main topics or main details, if any, then branch of it, and so on. When you ar finished, you would have an entire branch structure of all the subject matter. It is best to draw the entire structure before using the technique to memorize it. Also, you should re-draw it neatly, then save it for future reference.

I've read that when studying, retention level declines after a period o time. For the average person, it is about thirty minutes. In addition, the data most recallable is the first and last parts. I've read that it is due t a declining level of attention and concentration. This, I had noticed in myself before I've discovered this information. My theory of this has been that people tend, perhaps unconsciously, to try harder to memorize the first bits of information. They think that if they can remember th first parts, they can remember the rest. In addition to this, because th last bits have been received most recently, they are fresh in the mind Therefore, they are more recallable. Thus, is it easier to recall the first and last parts.

Nevertheless, it makes sense to experiment in order to find the time when your level of retention begins to decline. Then you would know the study and break interval best suited for yourself. It is said that a break should last at least 5 minutes. It is a good idea to do a recall of the material you have studied before continuing.

Many believe in listening to music when studying. I've found that o vocal music, the singing tends to be distracting. This is logical since the words sung are probably irrelevant to the subject matter. This can als apply to non vocal music of which the person trying to study knows the lyrics. However, I've found instrumental music that is soft and mellow t be beneficial to study

CHAPTER 28

ARTIFICIAL AND NATURAL ASSOCIATION

ARTIFICIAL ASSOCIATION

The type of association occurring throughout this book is an artificial association. Of this type, you form an association by creating a medium that connects the subjects. Three such mediums we have used are imaginary images, poems and acrostics. Artificial associations are obviously quite versatile and flexible.

NATURAL ASSOCIATION

Of natural associations, one or more mediums already exist. That is, you don't have to create anything if you know one or more such mediums.

For example, a natural association between alarm clock and radio is that the two are often combined to form one appliance. Another example is that between shoe and sneaker.

Often, a natural association is not so obvious. For example, I know that you can see at least two associations between rose and strawberry. One is that they are both plants. Another is that they are both red. However, an association that is not well known is that the two are genetically related.

As you probably can see, natural associations seem to be more permanent.

As you probably know, the use of natural associations are used often in the learning of a new language. As you also may know, the languages Spanish, French and English, for example, all evolved from the language Latin. Therefore, among these languages, many words of similar sounds are of similar meaning. Take, for instance, the English word *calorie*, which is the unit measurement of heat. From this, you could probably guess the meaning of the Spanish word *calor.*

Four good examples of the use of natural associations are in *Forming A Custom Peg System* on page 28. Also, you would find some examples in *Extending A Peg List* on page 26.

Chapter 29

MATHEMATICAL FORMULAS

Normally, I would have placed all the subject matter of this chapter within the chapter of *School and Technical Subjects.* Instead, I gave it its own chapter because it entails a great amount of subject matter.

You should skip this chapter if you do not have a good knowledge of algebra. In general, the techniques of this chapter are mainly for test situations. The best way to use the technique is to write the equation out on scrap paper as you decipher it from the technique. You should do this before you begin to apply it to the problem.

You can memorize a mathematical formula best by understanding it. That is, when the formula makes sense to you. You should use these techniques merely to verify that the equation as you think it should be, is correct. Therefore, I would first try to learn how the formula had been formed. Thus, I may learn how to construct the formula from scratch myself. To accomplish this, it is logical to try to learn about the formula from such sources as the text books and the teacher. Another way is to dissect the equation into its most discreet parts, then analyze it. Another is the apply certain numbers to it then analyze the results. Depending on the formula, one or more of these should be of great help. In finding how a formula had been formed, you would form natural associations. Therefore, you would increase recall power.

I recommend that you combine the Rote Method, your knowledge of how the formula had bed constructed and the memory technique. In this, you would have more than one form of the equation. With this, you could also use your recollection from one form to verify the information from one or more of the others.

As of most of the techniques in this book, the techniques of this chapter are ways of converting a mathematical formula into imaginary images and scenes for better recall. Now I will commence with the lessons on the memory systems.

One can apply the Link System or the Story Method with the alphabet and number images to a formula. You have probably thought of this yourself. For small formulas, this may suffice.

Take for instance, the following formula:

$$\frac{H}{t} = \frac{kA(t_1 - t_2)}{X}$$

One way to apply the story method is to imagine a story such as the following:

```
A telephone pole that always carries a tray with a ladder on
it (H/t) shares a bunk bed (=) with a pare of scissors (X).
The pair of scissors always carries a tray that has on it a
car jack (k), an easel (A) and a box. In the box, there are
```

```
            two smaller poles.  The tallest of  these poles  is  beating  a
            tree trunk, and the other is riding a swan.
```

If you visualize this story taking place as you apply the aspects we've learned in the beginning, you would probably have no difficulty recalling the details of this formula.

Another method for formulas is to first re-configure the formula into a serial form, then apply the Link System or the Story Method. A serial form is a form of which all characters are in a series from left to right. For example, I've re-configured the formula above to the following:

$$HX = tkA(t1 - t2)$$

Of course, instead of reconfiguring it, you could use slashes to put it into this serial form:

$$H / t = kA(t_1 - t_2) / X$$

The next step is to form mental images and scenes that link each symbol to the next and so on.

For chemical compounds, one can, of course, use the same methods. Another system to apply to chemistry is as follows. I will explain it by example using the following formula (formula of butane):

$$C_4 H_{10}$$

For this, I could use a system much like that for Two Dimensional Pegs (see Chapter 20 on page 68). For the first letter, C_4, I use the word *car*. As you can see, the r represents 4. To memorize this compound, you could apply the Link System to the series, *butane, car, hats*. The word butane causes me to think of a blue flame. Naturally it is my image for this word. For such a compound that has numbers in it, such as the 2 in 2nh3, One could memorize it using the series, *swan, Noah, ham*. Of course the *swan* depicts the number 2.

Of other functions, such as *sine, cosine, log,* and *in,* you can include them in a number of ways. One way is to derive a word for each. For instance, I use *sign* for *sin* and *coat sign* (imagine a street sign made of coat fabric) for *cosine*.

An idea I've just thought of is that it is not always necessary to depict unknowns and variables using images of letters. In these techniques, you can depict these using images of exactly what they are. For an example, let's consider the first formula of the chapter, which is on page 122. Let's suppose that the H depicts heat, t1 depicts initial time and t2 depicts ending time. My image of heat is that of a hot radiator. My image of initial time is a gun being shot pointed upwards to start a race. Finally, I see ending time as a ringing stop clock. I could simply use such images as these instead.

FOR MORE COMPLEX FORMULAS

To produce a more efficient system for long formulas, I've developed the following two systems. Although I find them satisfactory so far, I plan to continue their development. I am also developing other systems and all of this will be in the next edition of this book. These systems may seem complicated to learn initially. For both of these systems, you must establish in mind, a set of characters and rules. So far, it seems to me that any sophisticated memory system must involve this sort of adjustments. This is a good example why I say that children should learn such memory techniques. Thus, they would have already made such adjustments by the time they begin college. Before I begin, I must point out the following algebraic rules:

$$\sqrt[N]{A} = A^{\frac{1}{N}} \therefore \sqrt{A} = A^{\frac{1}{2}} = A^{.5}$$

$$A^{-N} = \frac{1}{A^N} \therefore A^{-1} = \frac{1}{A}$$

$$A \div B = \frac{A}{B} = A \cdot \frac{1}{B} = AB^{-1}$$

The symbol $\therefore$ depicts the word *therefore.* By using, manipulating, and combining any of these rules, I can find substitutes for certain symbols. In fact, I've never used the square root bracket ever since I've known these. With the use of these rules, you don't even have to use fractions. These rules add more flexibility in the way a person can configure an equation to apply it to the memory systems here. I suggest that you study them well at this point. I've included these rules for flexibility and because both systems do require re-configuring the formula into a serial form before applying it. Therefore, the methods I've mentioned before apply here as well.

A lso, I want you to keep in mind that for both systems, I depict subscripts and exponents using the up and down arrows. Note the following examples:

$A_N = A \downarrow N$ $\qquad\qquad A^N = A \uparrow N \quad A_N B = A \downarrow NB$

As you can see, such an arrow applies only to the very next character to it. There are but two exceptions. For one, to use but one arrow for more than one character, you could use parenthesis. For instance, an expression such as $A^{X-Y} B_1$ would be written as follows:

$$A \uparrow (X-Y) B \downarrow 1.$$

As this example shows, the up-arrow in this expression applies only to the characters within the parenthesis. For another example, a mathematical equation such as the following:

$$y = \int_{x=3}^{x=2} x^3 dx$$

for the purpose of applying it to the memory systems could be re-written as follows:

$$y = \int \uparrow(x=2) \downarrow(x=3) \; x \uparrow 3 \; dx$$

The other exception applies to an integer or letter that follows a minus sign, decimal point, or both, such as the following examples:

$$.7 \quad -7 \quad -.7 \quad -A$$

In such a case, the arrow applies to the integer or letter, including such preceding characters. Note the following examples:

$$A^{-U} = A\uparrow -U \quad A^{-5} = A\uparrow -5 \quad A^{-c}D = A\uparrow CU \quad A^{-5}8 = A\uparrow -.58$$

As you can see in the two examples on the right, the arrow applies to but one of the integers or letters. As for the rightmost example, it could be your choice whether the arrow applies to but one integer or both. However, whatever you decide, you must be consistent about your system.

Both systems also do not directly accommodate lowercase alphabet letters. The method I use to solve this problem is quite similar to the previous method (for exponents and subscripts). To indicate that an alphabet letter is of lowercase, precede the letter with a certain symbol that is to be used only for this purpose. The symbol I will use in both systems for this purpose is: ↘. To apply this method to the following expression: ABn + 2Nna. It would be written as follows: AB↘N + 2N↘N↘A. Notice that each letter to which it applies (lowercase letters) is preceded by that symbol. Therefore, the symbol applies only to the very next character to it.

The following is the only exception: To use but one such symbol for more than one letter, you could use parenthesis. For instance, the same expression could be written as follows: AB↘N + 2N↘(NA). Another option is that an expression such as $2n_2aN$ could be written as follows: ↘(2N42A)N. In this case, the symbol does apply only to the characters within the parenthesis. However, of those characters, it applies only to the alphabet letters. Bear this symbol in mind because it is mentioned again in both systems.

I derived the idea for this first memory system from both the Phonetic System and the Acrostic (Chapter 25). In summary, this system works by converting the formula, in portions, to short sentences of which one can form imaginary scenes. Then the person is to link these scenes together using the Link System. This linking is done by associating the last item in the sentence to the next scene. The system works as follows:

Of the sentences, each word depicts either a math symbol, an integer, an alphabet letter or a blank. As you may have guessed, blanks of this system serve the same purpose as they do in the Phonetic System. The following are the details:

- A word that is of the first peg list in Chapter 5 (Page 20) depicts that corresponding integer.

- A word that is not a noun, action verb (words such as is, are, and was are verbs, but not action verbs), or adjective is a blank. This includes adjectives such as first, other, and another. For better comprehension, try applying this rule to some of the sentences in this book, even to the very sentences you've just read.

- A word that doesn't apply to the 3 preceding rules, yet begins with one of the letters of the following chart, depicts its corresponding symbol in that chart (I've tried to assign each symbol to match its operation, such as division, open, close, top and bottom.).

- A word that is one of the alphabet words of Chapter 10 (page 37) depicts that corresponding letter.

. P	= E	(O	) C
+ A	- S	× M	÷ D
↑ T	↓ B	← L	→ R

All remaining words are blanks. Such words are nouns, action verbs, or adjectives. This includes words that don't apply to the first two rules above. Also, they do not begin with any of the 12 letters of the chart. You should note and memorize the letters not used, so that you can quickly find such blanks.

To add flexibility in constructing the sentences, you can form another set of alphabet and number image words, and use both sets of words together. You could use either a word from one set or the other set on a character. As you will see in the example, I use pyramid for A, coat hanger for 2, and totem pole for 1, as well as the words of the other alphabet list.

Because of the rules of the table above, a person could even eliminate certain symbols such as D and M. However, for flexibility, I don't recommend it. For more flexibility, I might eliminate E by depicting the equal sign as its image in the alphabet list (bunk bed). Thus I could use words beginning with E as blanks.

Yes, I realize that there are many details to remember for this system. This system would no doubt take some practice to learn.

Again, to include lowercase letters, I use the method described on page 125. To apply it to this system, the symbol used there (↘) is to have a corresponding word in this system. This word is to be used only for this purpose. The word I like best for this is *pawn*. *Pawn* reminds me of lowercase letters because the pawn is the lowest piece in the game Chess. For more flexibility, you could have more than one such word for this purpose.

And now for an example of the use of this system. Take the following equation:

$$X = \frac{7A_1^2 - 5A_2^2}{\sqrt{A^2 - 4BC}}$$

The first step is to re-configure it into a serial form, then re-write it using only the available symbols.

Of course, there are a number of ways to re-configure the equation. I've chosen the following form:

$$X = (7 A↓1↑2 - 5A↓2↑2)(A↑2 - 4 B C)↑ -.5$$

The next step is to change each character to its corresponding word or letter, as follows:

```
scissors e o street light easel b tree trunk t swan s hook
pyramid b swan t hanger c o pyramid t swan s sailboat
eyeglasses moon c t s p hook
```

The next step is to change the letters to words (non blanks) and insert blanks to form short sentences that you can visualize. Remember that the last item is always the first item in the next sentence. The following is of course only one of the possible series of sentences one could come up with:

```
A scissors is eating an orange street light as an easel
bites on a tree trunk that it has forcefully taken from a
swan. The swan stabs a hook into a pyramid's bottom as
another swan twists a hanger to cut an opening into the
pyramid. The pyramid is too tough for the swans so they
sail on a sailboat wearing eyeglasses as they howl at the
moon. The moon then cuts the top of the sail with a
pirate's hook.
```

At this point, you could go back to the first step to make changes to the configuration in order to form the type of words or sentences you want. For instance, I see some characters that you could omit. Likewise you could add characters to it as well.

The final step is to imagine these scenes taking place. Again, you should place a symbol of the purpose of the formula at the beginning. In this case, it is whatever X represents.

Provided you know the system well, recall of the equation should be no problem. Simply recall the scenes in their order. As you do this, write out each character from left to right. Finally, change each up or down arrow to the proper subscript or exponential form.

This next system, I've derived from the principles of binary and octal number conversions as taught on page 75, which is within Chapter 22. I will explain this system in the following steps:

I. **Setting up the system and mentally establishing it:**

   1. Establish a set of different characters and symbols of 100 or less. This set must consist of all 10 integers, all 26 alphabet letters, all math operation symbols, and other characters and symbols you might use.

   2. Put this entire series of characters and symbols into an order you can best memorize, then assign each character or symbol a different number according to its place in the series. Each number assignment must be a two digit number. This applies solely to the number assignments 0 to 9. For each of these, simply place a 0 to its left as a place holder. I suggest the following order:

NUMBER ASSIGNMENT	CHARACTER OR SYMBOL
O0toO9	Oto9
10	(decimal point)
11 to 36	A to Z
37to 40	+ - × ÷
41to44	↑ ↓ ← →
45 to 49	*sin cos tan inverse hyp*
50	=
51to64	≈ ≠ ∴ ( ) [ ] *log ln* , / | ; :
65 to 99	(other characters such as: π Σ ∫ Ω etc.)

Notice that the assignment of each alphabet letter is simply its normal place in the alphabet plus ten. For instance, if you already know that G is the seventh letter in the alphabet, to find its number assignment, simply add ten, thus deriving 17. Notice that I assigned 10 to the decimal point, and 50 to the equal sign. I did this because the decimal point reminds me of ten and the equal sign reminds me or the phrase "fifty fifty".

You do not necessarily have to use all 100 number assignments. As you can see . in the table, number assignments range from 00 to 99.

Number assignments not used can be used as blanks. As I will show later, such blanks can provide more flexibility in forming words and sentences.

Again, to include lowercase letters, I use the method described on page 125. To apply it to this system, the symbol used there (↘) is to have a corresponding number assignment in the chart. This number assignment is to be used only for this purpose. The number assignment I like best for this is 92 because it converts to *pawn* (Phonetic System). Again, *pawn* reminds me of lowercase letters because the pawn is the lowest piece in the game Chess. I prefer not to use up twenty six more number assignments just to accommodate the lowercase alphabet letters.

3. Memorize well each character's or symbol's number assignments. of course you can apply mnemonics such as the Peg System.

II. Applying the system to a formula.

1. First you must re-configure the formula into a serial form. Use only characters and symbols in your set. for instance let's apply the following formula:

$$W = \frac{B_1 - (A-B)^3 \sqrt{C_1}}{\sqrt{A+B-C}}$$

Again, there are many possible serial forms you could change it to. Nevertheless, I've re configured it to the following series:

$$W [B\downarrow 1 - (A-B)\uparrow 3x(C\downarrow 1)\uparrow .5] [A+B-C]\uparrow - .5$$

2. Convert each character or symbol to its assigned number. In doing this to the series above, I've derived the following:

33 50 56 12 42 01 38 54 11 38 12 55 41 03 39 54 13 42 01 55 41 10 05 57 56 11 37 12 38 13 57 41 64 38 10 05

Notice the last four numbers above, which are **64 38 10 05**. Let's suppose that the first of these four numbers, **64**, has no character assigned to it. I included this number to demonstrate the use of unassigned numbers as blanks. Later, in the lessons on recall of the formula, we will see the advantage of this.

3. Convert this series of numbers to words using the Phonetic Code System. It is not necessary to keep the digits in groups of two. Therefore, you can form such a word using any number of digits. I've derived the following series of words:

mummy, wool, slash, tinhorn, house, tomb, flare, totem, foot, nail, lord, Sam, ham, pillar, timer, nosedial, Willard, dice, locklatch, tooth, maggot, honey, muffet, mule, lard, charm, vats, sail

Of course, you could carefully select the groups and words to form a sentence. Applying this to part of the beginning of the series, I've derived the following:

A mummy will slash a tinhorn house to move a woolly rat. A dome of a tunnel will ride a sea mummy pillar…

At this point, you could go back to step 1 to change the series in order to form the type of words or sentences you want. For instance, I see a few characters in it that you could omit, including a pair of parenthesis. Likewise you could add characters to it as well.

Notice the third from last word, which is charm. This word was formed from the number I inserted as a blank, which is 64, and the 3 of the next number, which is 38. Thus, I demonstrate the use of blanks to add flexibility in the choice of words.

4. memorize this series of words by applying the Link System or the Story Method. Remember to place at the beginning, an image to remind you what the formula is for.

III. Using the system to recall the formula:

Simply do the reverse process, such as the following steps:

1. Recall the series of words by recalling the images and scenes you had imagined.

2. As you recall the words; convert them back to numbers and write the numbers down.

4. Convert each group to its corresponding symbol or character and write it down. Of course, you discard any numbers that are blanks. Thus, you would have reconstructed the serial form of the formula.

As I've implied, the system employs the principles of binary and octal conversions. There is only one real difference here. Binary and octal numbers are of base 2 or 8. Well, this system is like converting a number from base 100 to base 10, or visa versa. In this system, you start with a series that consists of up to 100 characters. then you convert this series down to a series consisting of only 10 different characters.

Perhaps an easier way to apply a formula to this system is with the use of a table. For this, first form a table such as that below, on lined paper such as graph paper. To demonstrate this method, I've applied this simple equation to the table below:

$$X = (A+M)(M-R) \uparrow -2$$

Notice that I've placed its characters in the *character* column (cmi.) in descending order.

CHR.	#ASSN.	BLANKS	WORDS
		95	plu
X	34	91	Mer, ped
=	50	99 91	els, pop bott-
(	54	94	le, robber
A	11		tooth,
+	37	95	mug, poll-
M	23		en, mu-
)	55	90	le, lip, pa-
(	54		il, ri-
M	23		no, mu
-	38		mmy, fa
R	28	69	n, fudge, pil-
)	55		l, la-
↑	41	74	rd, cru-
-	38	64 91	m, fish, robot
2	02	74	sneaker

In the *number assignment* column (# ASSN.), I've written beside each character its assigned number. In the *blanks* column, I place any unassigned numbers I choose to use as blanks (For this demonstration, let's assume that numbers 60 through 100 are unassigned).

Notice the row above the first character, which is there to accommodate blanks before the first character's place number. Of course, the numbers of any row are to be read straight across from the *number assignment* column to the blanks column. As you can see in the *words* column, I've divided some words using dashes. This, I did so that every letter is in the same row as its corresponding number.

The advantage of using such a table is that there is plenty of room for experimenting with blanks and words.

CHAPTER 30

ADVICE

To reinforce recall of any of the scenes and images, one must either use them or mentally review them periodically. The interval between reviews should be at most about five times each time a review is done. For example, the first interval may be a day. The next may be a week. Then it's a month. Then it's five months and so on. You could do a mental review at any time you are doing nothing that would distract you. It is a good idea to review new information at the end of the day. One way to handle this is with the use of system comprising of written records. If you are a computer user, you could use a computer for such records. Another way is to mentally link each subject you want to periodically review, using the Link System. Then you can review these linking scenes to prevent your forgetting to review one or more of the subjects. In addition, you can continuously add subjects to the links. You can have more than one linking list.

With the use of the techniques throughout this book, you could be developing mental and career skills at idle times of which you don't have the opportunity to study. For instance, let's consider a security guard who must stay at a post of which he can do nothing but sit or stand. Using memory techniques, this guard could be reviewing study material and information he had memorized using the techniques. I myself found this quite useful.

It is helpful to create and use more than one association to the information for later recall. This provides options, which increases your chances of recalling the information. Then if you find that one of the associations you created to the information doesn't help you to later recall it, you could then try recalling using the other ways or associations you form to it. Chanced are that one or more will work and each form would help you to recall the others, thus re-enforcing all of them.

Most people memorize information by repeatedly reviewing or recalling it until its recall becomes easy. This method is the Rote Memory Method. Obviously, it is not so quick and effective as the techniques in this book. Nevertheless, I advise that you always apply the Rote Method to information memorized using the techniques. As I've stated in the beginning, the best way to use the techniques is merely to verify information.

In using the Rote Method in this way, you strengthen the establishment of new memory patterns. For example, for a telephone number you apply, recall it from the image you have formed to record it. Then you repeat the digits to yourself at times. Thus, you would store it in more than one form and soon you wouldn't need to recall the mnemonic image again.

It is quite possible to use more than one memory strategy for an application consisting of listed details. For each listed detail, you can decide which memory technique to use on it. An example of this is in the chapter about codes, particularly the four Morse Code Systems. Another good example is the common method to memorize the Phonetic Code System (Page 44).

As I've stated, most of the systems are adaptable to other interests. For instance, I can think of a number of different applications to the techniques taught in the chapter of playing cards. For instance, a supervisor can use the mutilation idea (page 70) to keep track of the status of tasks in a large schedule.

If you are like most people, you can experiment and create your own systems for such applications as those in this book. Some of the systems and enhancements of systems in this book, I've created as I wrote it. Because of the extensive use of the imagination, the use of the systems exercises the imagination. Thus, they increase creativity. There are good books on creative thinking. One book I recommend is *A whack on the side of the head.*

The use of artificial associations (see page 121) is often an inadequate substitute for a good understanding of the subject matter at hand. As I had said in the beginning, information that makes sense to you, you can recall more easily. This is even better when it occurs without the need for mnemonics. This, you would achieve by the accumulation of other related information. In the process of this accumulation, you find natural associations. Thus, you build on already existing memory patterns. You should always try to replace artificial associations with natural associations.

Nevertheless, the technique would help you to recall the information until such integration of knowledge takes place, and for tests. As you would agree, most tests are given before you understand the subject matter. This is because our education system to this day is fallible in many areas, which includes teaching methods and lesson plans. Some believe that such flaws are intentionally placed there so that only a few would undergo the entire discipline.

Besides, there are some types of information that do not have natural associations. For instance, suppose that you are requires to be able to recall from memory any writings in the Bible. For example, suppose that you had to recall from memory what is Chapter 18, verse 7, of the book of John in the Bible. The point I'm trying to make here is that such a chapter and verse number has no natural association with that text there. For another example, suppose that a law student had to be able to recall the details of any of many laws if given its article and section number. Other examples of such information are the Morse Code, police radio codes, etc., etc., etc.

Therefore, the techniques are a valuable asset regardless. It is impractical to try to memorize a large clump of information, or to do anything for that matter no matter how small, without some sort of system.

Organization is very important in any memorization task. As you know, any items put away in an unorganized fashion would probably be difficult to find later. This applies to information as well, which is the reason for such aids as file systems. Likewise, it applies to memorization, which pertains to finding information in the brain. Therefore, as I've just said, one should use a system. One advantage of using such memory techniques as those in this books is that it provides a means of organizing information in the brain.

Attitude affects memorization ability:

If you notice, information that is not of interest to you or unimportant to you, you will tend to lose the ability to recall. The brain knows when this is so and responds by eliminating that which enables you to recall it.

Many people have detrimental ideas about their memory abilities. One such idea is that they can possibly run out of memory space. It is not so It would take more than one lifetime to fill even a tenth of ones memory space.

Another wrong and detrimental idea is that the brain works less during idle times, and more during times of diligent studying. This is not so, because the brain is constantly adsorbing info from all of its senses (sight, sound, touch, etc.). This is so whether you're studding a book, or doing nothing, such as staring at an empty wall. In other words, the brain is constantly recording, and there is no way to turn this recorder off. The only possible exception is during sleep.

Often people who believe in such detrimental ideas unknowingly cripple their own memory abilities For instance, unwittingly, and out of habit, they resist memorizing information. Thus, they unwittingly train themselves to forget. Then their acquired abilities to forget encourages these beliefs even more. Furthermore, they don't test and exercise their memorization abilities.

Often, the inability to recall information in not only a problem of recall. It's an attentiveness problem as well. Of course, one should always pay attention and try to improve ones memorization skills.

It is very important to trust your memory, and I cannot stress this point enough. Many times, I had successfully recalled information I needed. However, because I didn't trust in my memorization abilities, I had assumed that the information is wrong. This, I had done without wiving it ant thought. This of course has a negative effect on memory. It retards one.s development in using it. As you practice memorization, you should also practice such trust to allow such underestimated abilities to work to their fullest potential.

My point in all this is as I 've stated, attitude affects memorization ability.

An experiment depicted in an article in Developmental Psychology, volume 25, of 1989 indicated that a negative estimation of ones memorization abilities has an adverse effect. The article also indicates that memory ability does not deteriorate with age. It states that a weaker ability is usually due to attitude. It also states that it's due to beliefs about memory and lack of memory use.

I've learned of certain nutrients that enhance the brains performance in such areas as memory. The most prominent of these are two herbs named Gotu Kola and L-Glutomine. The following are two brain formulas according to the book, Herbally yours.

Cayenne, Gotu Kola, Ginseng.

Bayberry, Black Walnut, Comfrey, Fennel, Ho Show-Wum, Licorice, Peppermint, Bee pollen, Cayenne, Eucalyptus, Gentian, Lemon pass, Myrrh.

The book contains information about all known herbs and their uses. The book *Brain Boosters, Foods that make you smart* is another good source of information on nutients for enhancements of mental abilities

I've also read that substances that block arteries, such as cholesterol, impair the brain's functioning and therefore effect memory.

It is the opinion of some, including other authors of publications pertaining to this topic, that some of the available mnemonic techniques are not worth learning. According to them, it is more of a hassle to learn certain techniques then it is to apply simpler or more conventional memory methods. This would be so if the user of the technique planned to use it on but one application only.

However, the user would probably use such a mnemonic technique on many applications throughout his or her life. By the continued use of the technique on a wide variety of applications, the user automatically masters the technique easily. As I've implied in the beginning of this book, one should never assume that another is always correct. This applies to authors, doctors, and other such professionals as well.

It is probable that such people, as they previewed some of the mnemonic techniques in other books, assumed that they are too complicated to be of practical use. Then to make matters worse, these authors probably didn't test these techniques well, to see if such assumptions were true. This, course of action you should always try to avoid. Even if such a method initially seems too complicated for your use, you should never assume that it is. Instead, you should give it a good try. For this, simply ask yourself: What is there to lose by trying it?

Also, you should never let another person persuade you not to try an idea. That is, of course if there's no substantial risk in trying it. For this, ask your self the same question: what is there to lose by trying it?

However, some of the techniques do require learning certain systems and codes. This is another good reason for children to learn such techniques. The most appropriate time is during elementary and intermediate school.

When working towards a goal, one should never dwell on what someone has already accomplished. When studying, one should never study what one already knows. This puts progress to a halt. In most cases, it is dues to habit. For good advice of ambition, I recommend the books, *Think and Grow Rich*, and *Secrets of Mind Power*.

As I've said, the mind works with patterns. Therefore, as I've stated, one should use a system in all one's endeavors. After all, every creation from the very beginning has occurred using some sort of system. One should determine ones life priorities then categorize them into levels. Then one should govern one's life according to them, without deviation. Such deviation and cause one to falter.

If you have a problem of which mnemonics is a possible solution, Send me an email message about it. My email address is: JIC60@yahoo.com. Perhaps I could be of help. I appreciate any sort of input. I might even develop a new memory technique for that particular application.

FORGETFULNESS PROBLEMS

As I've shown you can use Memory Techniques to help remind you of important tasks or items. However, the use of a mnemonic is not always the best sollutin for such problems. For these, there are other methods one could use of which one can easily derive from common sense. For instance, you can solve such problems by simply forming and developing beneficial habits.

Although this may not exactly cure you of the forgetfulness itself, it would eliminate the undesirable effects. The following are some methods.

So that you make sure that you take with you a certain item on your trip tomorrow, put the item with , in, or on top of another item you know you will remember to take. This item could be something such as your keys, hat or purse. Your keys, for example, you probably couldn't leave, even if you did initially forget them, because you need them to lock your door behind you, or start your car. I use a similar system in my daily routine. I always place such important items in a certain tray, along with my keys. I never place such items anywhere else, ever. Another such system is to place important items at the door you plan to leave from. Thus, you will see the items on your way out.

This not only pertains to leaving the household, It pertains to other places as well. For instance, I use a similar system to assure that I would not leave items in such a place as a bus, train, or restaurant. I'm so used to carrying around my briefcase that I'm in the habit of looking for it and taking it just before leaving. Therefore, I know that it quite unlikely that I'll ever leave it. In my briefcase, is a looped boot string which is run through a small hole in a divider inside, then tied end to end. To prevent leaving such items as, for example, a wet umbrella, I close the briefcase with part of the string sticking out. Then I form a loop on this outside end, put the umbrella handle through the loop, then pull on the string to tighten the loop around it a bit. Thus, the umbrella is attached to the briefcase to prevent my leaving it behind.

When using such systems It's good practice not to ever delay in applying it. Don't put it off, not even for a moment, because there's a chance that you might forget to apply it.

Another way to avoid forgetfulness problems is to keep in mind the number of items or tasks. For instance, before your trip to town, you could keep in mind the number of items you- plan to take with you or purchase. If you do this, you probably will not leave the house or store until you have recalled and assembled every item in that number. For another example, as you prepare for the day, you keep in mind the number of tasks you plan to perform. Likewise, you will successfully try to recall each of the tasks.

Chapter 31

THE GALLERY

I've chosen to call this chapter *The Gallery* or should I say *The Art Gallery*. This chapter contains the illustrations I've mentioned in one of the beginning chapters of this book. These pictures are some of the scenes I've described in the lessons throughout this book as I've imagined them. As I've said, I have not placed these illustrations with the text that pertains to them. In addition, I've purposely excluded any references as to the location of such text.

Again, My reason for separating these from the text is that I want you the reader to exercise your own imagination and creativity. This is essential to the comprehension of this book. If I were to provide at hand an illustration every time I describe an imaginary scene, the reader would most likely think of the illustrated scene instead of creating his or her own mental scene from scratch. As I've stated, I feel that such pictures could even be detrimental to your progress in this book if you do not exercise your own creativity.

I therefore leave it to you to guess and figure out the location of the text that pertains to any of these pictures if you so wish to. It could even be a fun motivating game to play while reading the book. That is of course, if you look at the pictures before beginning any of the lessons. Also, such quessing after studying any of the books lessons could help in recalling the lessons, which can result in better learning.

As I have stated, I've included these pictures merely to add interest and color to the book and to display my art work. I think that the artwork is pretty good considering that I've never known that I could do any art like this. I feel that this ability is due to my practicing the memory techniques. As I've said in the beginning, practicing the techniques develops creativity as well as other mental functions. As a result of this new ability, I now study art and work to improve my skill at it.

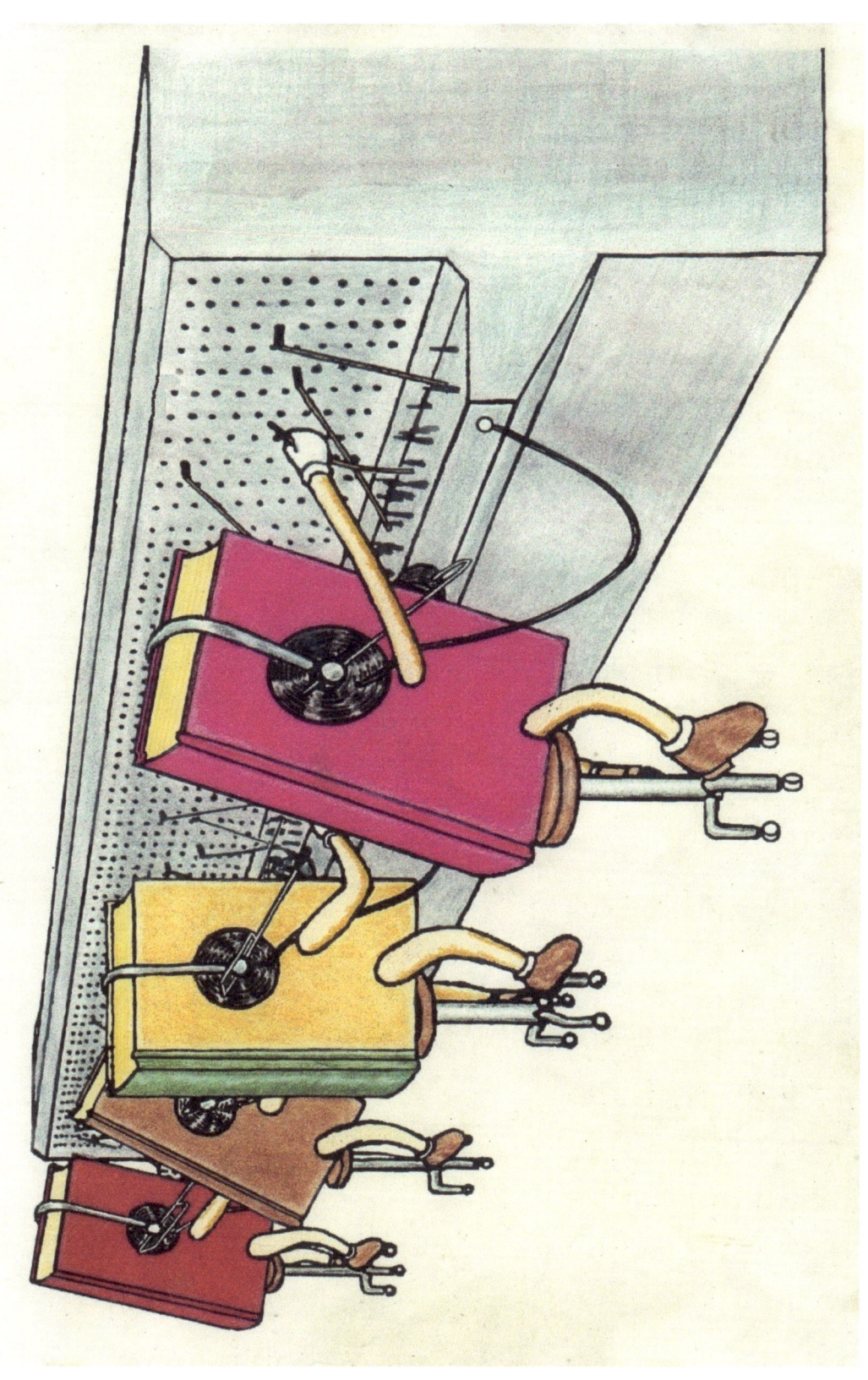

141

145

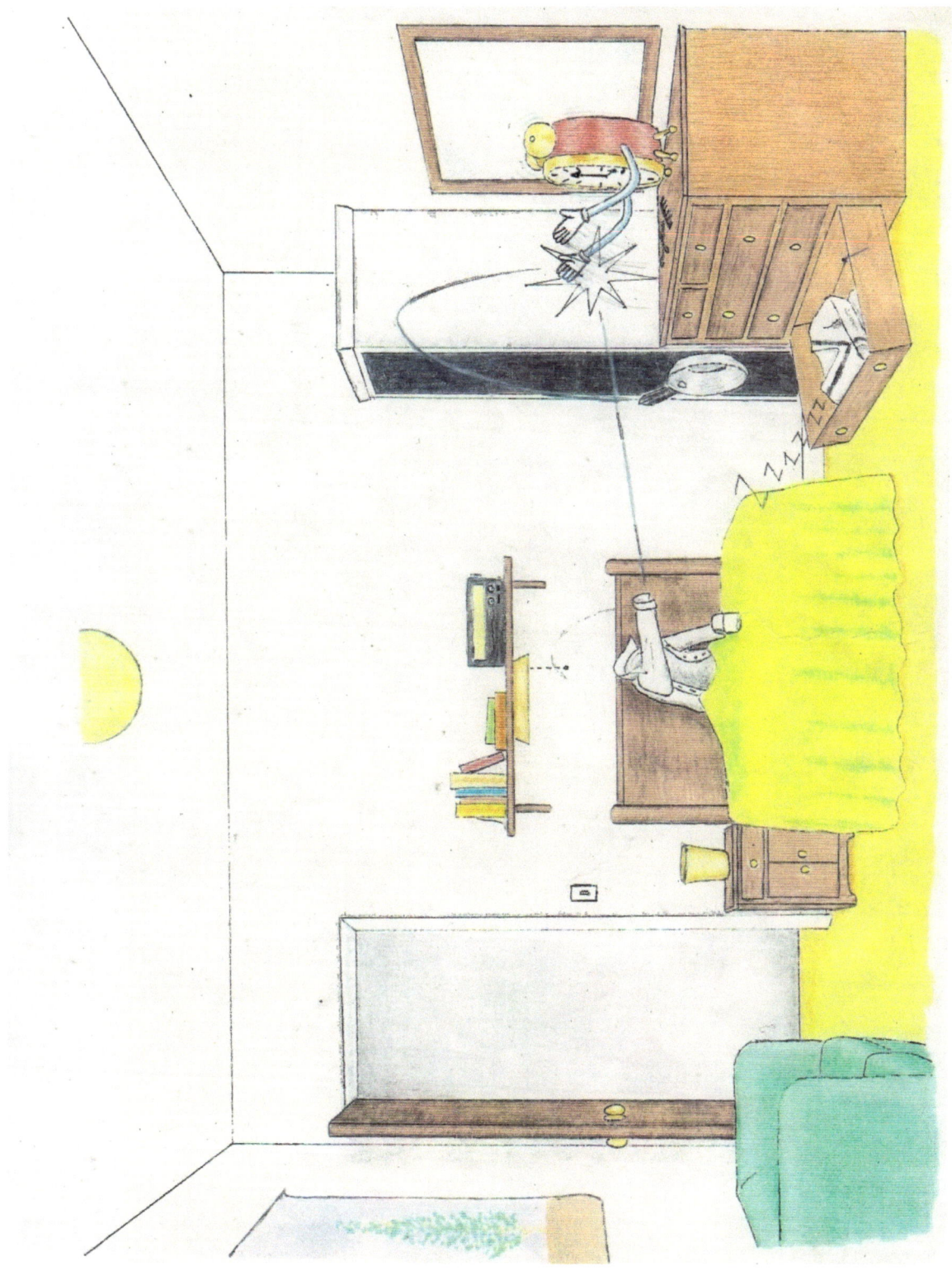

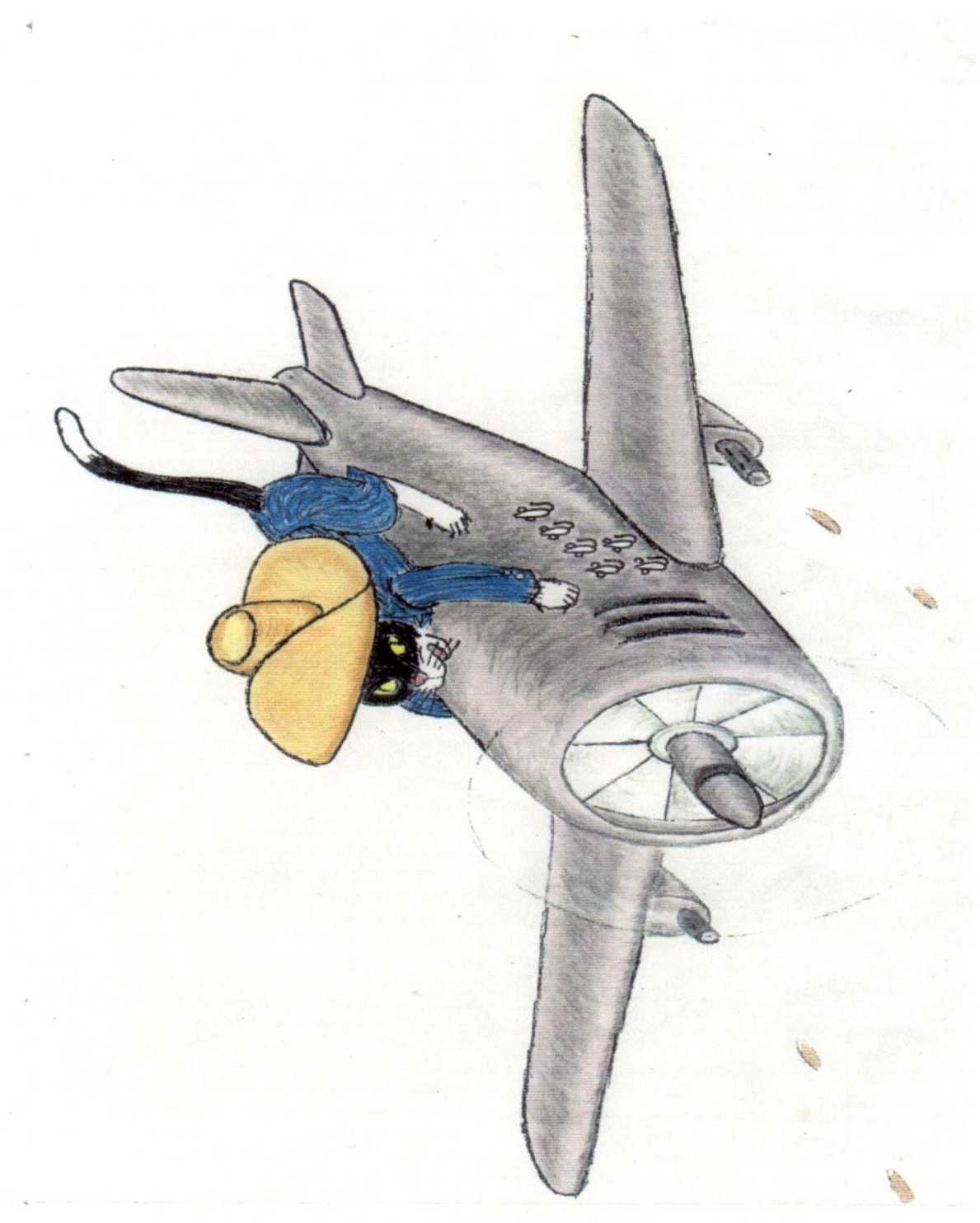

ANSWERS TO EXERCISES

CHAPTER 15

I.

1. 7462
2. 621532
3. 944
4. 09427
5. 0582
6. 405
7. 7014762
8. 256
9. 34620
10. 10740
11. 075675
12. 84272012
13. 6401762
14. 472020
15. 3140
16. 705462
17. 1062
18. 1084
19. 284362
20. 62
21. 4846462
22. 0765
23. 02187
24. 274
25. 74748
26. 74030
27. 7494714
28. 82265
29. 95
30. 114
31. 3212
32. 6392

33. 14740294752
34. 28478074282947
36. 9200910118321
36. 41114174982
37. 9412108121070104147
38. 219112111810

II

1. J or T
2. L
3. E or G
4. C, M, or N
5. K
6. D
7. I
8. B or R
9. H
10. A or F
11. Q
12. P
13. S
14. K
15. E or G
16. I
17. J or T
18. Q
19. A or F
10. S

CHAPTER 19

1. Tues
2. Thurs
3. Tues
4. Sat
5. Tues
6. Fri
7. Sun
8. Thurs
9. Sun
10. Mon
11. Fri
12. Fri
13. Sun
14. Mon
15. Mon
16. Fri
17. Mon
18. Fri
19. Fri
20. Sat
21. Thurs
22. Fri
23. Mon
24. Tues
25. Sun
26. Wed
27. Sun
28. Sun
29. Wed
30. Fri
31. Thurs
32. Wed

CHAPTER 22

1. 111101100001(2)
2. 260(8)
3. 111000001000(2)
4. 1155(8)
5. 1010011100(2)
6. 1101(8)
7. 111100111(2)
8. 100011010001(2)
9. 1000001001(2)
10 511(8)
11. 3276(8)
12. 1612(8)
13. 137(8)
14. 147(8)
15. 11001111011(2)

BIBLIOGRAPHY

Bart L. Benne:	*Waspleg and Other Mnemonics*: Taylor 1988: Dallas, Tex
Eric M. Bienstock:	*Success Through Better Memory*: Perigee 1989: N.Y.C.
William G. Browning:	*Memory Power for Exams*: Cliffs Notes 1983: Lincoln, Na.
Tony Buzan:	*Use Both Sides of Your Brain*: E. P. Dutton 1976: N.Y.C.
"	*Use Your Perfect Memory*: E. P. Dutton 1984: N.Y.C.
Bruno Furst:	*Stop Forgetting:* Double Day 1972: Garden City, N.Y.
Napoleon Hill and Dennis Kimbro:	*Think and Grow Rich*: a Black Choice: Ballentine 1991: N.Y.C.
Steven Jacobson:	*Mind Control in the United States*: Critique Publishing: 1985: Santa Rosa, Ca.
Harry Lorayne:	*Remembering People:* Stein & Day 1975: N.Y.C.
"	*Secrets of Mind Power*: Signet 1975: N.Y.C.
"	*Super Memory-Super Student*: Little Brown 1990: Boston, Mass.
"	*The Memory Book:* Stein and day 1974: N.Y.C.
Kevin Trudeau	*Mega Memory*: Nightingale Conant Corp 1990: Wheeling, IL.
Ra U Nefer Amen:	*Metu Neter, Vol. 1:* Khaniit 1990: N.Y.C.
Nur Ankr Amin:	*The Ankr:* Nur Ankr Amin Co.: 1993: Jamaica, N.Y.
Roger Von Oech:	*A Whack on the Side of the Head*: Warner 1990: N.Y.C.
Beverly Potter and Sabastian Orfari:	*Brain Boosters: Foods That Make You Smart*: Ronin Publishing 1993: Berkely, Ca.
Joel A. Rodgers:	*Your History* : Black Classic Press 1983: Baltimore MD.
Penny C. Royal:	*Herbally Yours:* Sound Nutrition 1991: Hurricane, Utah.

PERIODICALS

George Rebok & Laurie Balcerak: *Memory Self Efficacy and Performance Differences*: Developmental psychology, Vol. 25,5: 1989

Lin Grensing: *Information processing:* About...Time: Oct., 1989

(This manuscript is copyright registered by the U.S.-L.O.C.)

ORDER FORM

memorytechniques.net

JIC60@YAHOO.COM

www.ingramcontent.com/pod-product-compliance
Lightning Source LLC
Chambersburg PA
CBHW041514220426
43668CB00002B/20